JESUS AND THE GOSPEL OF THOMAS

LOCHLAINN SEABROOK WRITES IN THE FOLLOWING GENRES

American Civil War
American History
American Politics
American South
Ancient History
Biblical Exegesis
Biblical Hermeneutics
Biography
Christian Mysticism
Coffee Table
Comparative Mythology
Comparative Religion
Cooking
Diet and Nutrition
Education
Ethnic Studies
Etymology
European History
Exposés
Family Histories
Film
Genealogy
Ghost Stories
Health and Fitness
Humor
Law of Attraction
Life After Death
Matriarchy
Men
Metaphysics
Military History
Mysteries and Enigmas
Natural Health
Natural History
Onomastics
Paleography
Paranormal
Patriarchy
Philosophy
Photography
Poetry
Politics
Presidential History
Quiz
Reference
Religion
Revolutionary Period
Science
Self-help
Spirituality
Spiritualism
Technology
Thanatology
Thealogy
Theology
UFOlogy
Victorian Period
Wildlife
Women
World History

Mr. Seabrook does not author books for fame and glory, but for the love of writing and sharing his knowledge.

SeaRavenPress.com

JESUS AND THE GOSPEL OF
THOMAS

*A Christian Mystic's View
of Christianity's Most Important Ancient Text*

BY

LOCHLAINN SEABROOK
AUTHOR, HISTORIAN, ARTIST

Diligently Researched and Generously Illustrated
by the Author for the Elucidation of the Reader

2025

Sea Raven Press, Park County, Wyoming, USA

JESUS AND THE GOSPEL OF THOMAS

Published by
Sea Raven Press, LLC, Founded 1995
Cassidy Ravensdale, President
Park County, Wyoming, USA
SeaRavenPress.com

Copyright © all text and illustrations Lochlainn Seabrook 2025
in accordance with U.S. and international copyright laws and regulations, as stated and protected under the Berne Union for the Protection of Literary and Artistic Property (Berne Convention), and the Universal Copyright Convention (the UCC). All rights reserved under the Pan-American and International Copyright Conventions.

PRINTING HISTORY
1st SRP paperback edition, 1st printing, April 2025 • ISBN: 978-1-955351-53-9
1st SRP hardcover edition, 1st printing, April 2025 • ISBN: 978-1-955351-54-6

ISBN: 978-1-955351-53-9 (paperback)
Library of Congress Control Number: 2025936032

This work is the copyrighted intellectual property of Lochlainn Seabrook and has been registered with the Copyright Office at the Library of Congress in Washington, D.C., USA. No part of this work (including text, covers, drawings, photos, illustrations, maps, images, diagrams, etc.), in whole or in part, may be used, reproduced, stored in a retrieval system, or transmitted, in any form or by any means now known or hereafter invented, without written permission from the publisher. The sale, duplication, hire, lending, copying, digitalization, or reproduction of this material, in any manner or form whatsoever, is also prohibited, and is a violation of federal, civil, and digital copyright law, which provides severe civil and criminal penalties for any violations.

Jesus and the Gospel of Thomas: A Christian Mystic's View of Christianity's Most Important Ancient Text, by Lochlainn Seabrook. Includes an index, illustrations, endnotes, and a bibliography.

ARTWORK
Front and back cover design and art, book design, layout, font selection, and interior art by Lochlainn Seabrook.
All images, image captions, graphic design, and graphic art copyright © Lochlainn Seabrook.
All images selected, placed, manipulated, cleaned, colored, tinted, and/or created by Lochlainn Seabrook.
Cover image: Jesus Walking on Water Along the Shore of the Sea of Galilee, circa 28 A.D.

All persons who approve of the authority and principles of Colonel Lochlainn Seabrook's literary work, and realize its benefits as a means of reeducating the world about facts left out of mainstream books, are hereby requested to avidly recommend his titles to others and to vigorously cooperate in extending their reach, scope, and influence around the globe.

The views documented in this book concerning Jesus, the Gospel of Thomas, & early Christian history are those of the publisher.

WRITTEN, DESIGNED, PUBLISHED, PRINTED, & MANUFACTURED IN THE UNITED STATES OF AMERICA

Dedication

Epigraph

"That is the true faith which is most ancient, and that a corruption which is modern."

Tertullian

160 A.D. to 240 A.D.

CONTENTS

Notes to the Reader, by Lochlainn Seabrook ❧ page 11

CHAPTER 1: THE GOSPEL OF THOMAS UP CLOSE ❧ page 15
CHAPTER 2: TEXT OF THE GOSPEL OF THOMAS ❧ page 51
CHAPTER 3: INTRODUCTION ❧ page 69
ANCIENT TEXT WITH MYSTICAL INTERPRETATIONS ❧ page 77

Notes ❧ page 117
Bibliography ❧ page 123
Index ❧ page 133
Praise for the Author ❧ page 149
Meet the Author ❧ page 151
Learn More ❧ page 153

Ancient Egypt: Birthplace of both traditional and mystical Christianity.

"Books invite all; they constrain none."
Hartley Burr Alexander (1873-1939)

NOTES TO THE READER

"NOTHING IN THE PAST IS DEAD TO THE MAN WHO WOULD
LEARN HOW THE PRESENT CAME TO BE WHAT IT IS."
WILLIAM STUBBS, VICTORIAN ENGLISH HISTORIAN

☞ Throughout this book I use the word "Thomas" as an abbreviation of the book the Gospel of Thomas. However, I use the personal name "St. Thomas" to indicate the actual historical figure of the Apostle known by that name.

☞ The secrets and mysteries I have revealed in this book do not begin to scratch the surface of Christian mysticism. They represent only a microscopic fraction of the arcane knowledge that exists in the vast library of mystical Christianity. I encourage those who are interested in this topic to read my many other books on spirituality, religion, and mythology, listed in my bibliography.

Lochlainn Seabrook
Rocky Mountains, USA
April 2025
In Nobis Regnat Christus

"Split a log; I am there.
Lift the stone, and you
will find me there."

The Christ (Christ Consciousness) speaking
through the human form known as Jesus

From the Gospel of Thomas

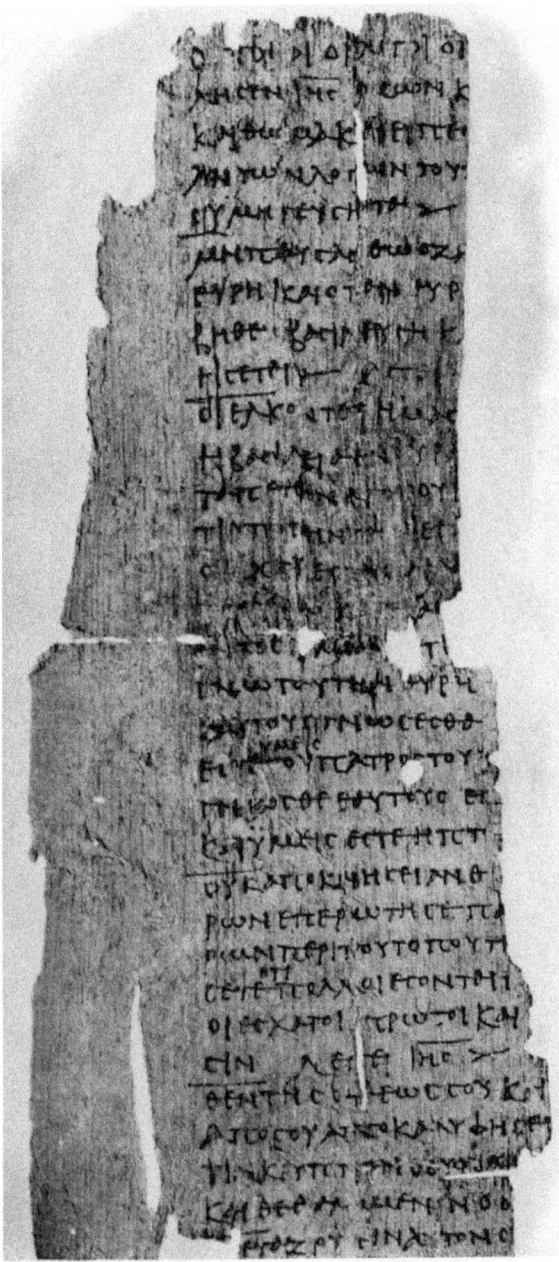

Original fragment from the Oxyrhynchus Gospel of Thomas.

Columns in ancient Egypt's great Hall of Karnak.

CHAPTER ONE
THE GOSPEL OF THOMAS UP CLOSE

ENDLESS ENIGMAS AND CONUNDRUMS surround the Gospel of Thomas: The author is unknown, the writer or speaker is unknown, the precise date of authorship is unknown, the original language is unknown, the location of authorship is unknown, its theological position is unknown, its Christology is unknown, the intended audience is unknown, its purpose is unknown, whether it was written for private or public usage is unknown, and finally whether it is an original (independent) or derivative (extracted) text is unknown.

We would like to know, for example, if it was written by a Gnostic Christian or an orthodox Christian, or a different sort of Christian, perhaps a Christian pantheist. Did Jesus actually utter the words in Thomas as claimed, or were they later unceremoniously appended to him by a well-intentioned scribe or Christian group? There is a Greek version and a Coptic version of Thomas, both sharing similarities, yet punctuated with overt differences. Which, if either, is the original version and which is a copy, and which is the most accurate? What was the original language of Thomas: Greek, Egyptian, Hebrew, Latin, Semitic, Syriac, or Aramaic, or something else entirely?

Why does Thomas contain theological discrepancies, and even contradictory material within its pages? Was Thomas written as a single document by a single individual at one sitting, or, like the Gospel of Q, was it composed by numerous people in various phases over time? Was it created merely to preserve some of Jesus' teachings, or did it have a didactic purpose—or both? Was the Gospel of Thomas intended to describe the inner (esoteric) meaning of Jesus' words to an elite group of spiritually evolved followers, or was it meant to be read and understood literally by the unenlightened masses? These and hundreds of other questions continue to be asked, nearly all still without definitive answers, and none with any unifying consensus among scholars.[1]

In short, the provenance of the Gospel of Thomas is a complete mystery. It stands alone on an empty page in history with no established author, no time period, no background—only what we can glean from it based on modern scholarship, personal knowledge, common sense, and intuition.

Despite this, we currently have more fragments of this Gospel in hand than we do of the canonical Gospel of Mark, for example.[2] What does it all mean? In this book I will fit as many pieces of the jigsaw puzzle together as possible.

Ancient Egypt: Probable birthplace of the Gospel of Thomas.

DISCOVERY

Like a number of other lost ancient texts, the Gospel of Thomas was not discovered by one individual as a single complete book. Rather it was gradually discovered by a number of people one fragment at a time, after which it was painstakingly pieced together over many years.

An initial papyrus fragment of eight sayings, known as "Papyrus Oxyrhynchus 1," was found by Bernard P. Grenfell and Arthur S. Hunt in 1897 in a rubbish mound in the ruins of the ancient Egyptian city of Oxyrhynchus—part of which today is occupied by the modern town of El-Bahnasa (or Behnesa). Much of the leaf they found was in a severely deteriorated state with ragged edges, holes, faded writing, and obviously missing lines. It was clearly from a small book of some kind, one known as a codex: a manuscript in book form, usually associated with sacred scripture or classical history.

While as many as 10 lines seemed to be missing from the leaf, the eight surviving lines were just enough to determine that the anonymous author had recorded the purported words of Jesus. One scholar described the find this way: We appear to have before us "a leaf from an ancient cheap and portable copy" of sayings attributed to Jesus.[3] Meanwhile, that same year Grenfell and Hunt published their meager but exciting find in a small book entitled, *Logia Iesou: Sayings of Our Lord, From an Early Greek Papyrus.*

A second papyrus fragment, labeled "Papyrus Oxyrhynchus 654," was found by the same two scholars during a subsequent excavation in 1903 at the same location. Deriving from a roll rather than from a codex, it contained an additional five sayings, but was quite damaged and nearly unreadable. A third fragment, "Papyrus Oxyrhynchus 655," also discovered by Grenfell and Hunt at Oxyrhynchus, was unearthed in 1903. In 1904 they published a second book on their latest findings entitled, *New Sayings of Jesus and Fragment of a Lost Gospel.*

Being only pieces of obviously larger works, it was not at first clear how these three fragments were related; though it was apparent to paleographers and codicologists that they were copies of an identical volume.

Making things more difficult, the fragmented leaves contained numerous doublets, accretions, deletions, additions, interpolations, emendations, abbreviations, repetitions, eccentricities, contradictions, transpositions, duplications, lack of punctuation marks, scribal mistakes, and most serious of all, possible mistranslations. These issues left a host of cryptic lacunae in the text that have continued to baffle experts, hindering a full and complete understanding of Thomas.

Nonetheless, many mysteries began to clear away as of December 1945, when a fortuitous event occurred in the region of Nag Hammadi, a city in Upper Egypt. It was here that a veritable "library" of ancient Coptic texts[4] (originally composed in Greek) was accidently discovered by two Egyptian peasants who were digging in the sand for nitrate at the base of a fallen boulder. Stored in a jar, the precious find included 12 (some say 13) leather-bound codices (books) filled with 52 tractates, probably deposited there around 400 A.D.[5] The Nag Hammadi Library, a stunning archaeological find that spanned a period of over 500 years, included a seemingly complete version of Thomas, one later named the "Coptic Gospel of Thomas." For the first time, the three original Greek fragments were seen to be part of the same larger work now known simply as the Gospel of Thomas.[6]

Nag Hammadi, Egypt: Discovery site of the complete Gospel of Thomas.

WHAT IS THE GOSPEL OF THOMAS?

Thomas, which some scholars are calling "the most important document discovered at Nag Hammadi,"[7] is a "free compilation"[8] of the sayings of Jesus, a collection known variously as logoi ("words"), logia ("oracles"), proverbs, aphorisms, epigrams, adages, or apothegms. The ancient work also includes a number of the Master's prophecies and parables.

Some suggest that due to its authoritative spiritual nature, Thomas would have been more correctly entitled "The Solemn Utterances of Jesus" rather than "The Words [Sayings] of Jesus," a title these particular individuals regard as an "inadequate translation" of the Greek word λόγια, meaning "words."[9] Either way, Evelyn-White accurately describes Thomas as "a series of short, independent Sayings without any connections, either of narrative or (apparently) of subject."[10]

The Logia of Jesus, first series, recto. Dimensions: 3¾" wide, 5¾" high; discovered in 1897 at Oxyrhynchus, Egypt, by Grenfell and Hunt.

Intriguingly, 2,000 years ago St. Paul referenced an assemblage of special "oracles"—divine teachings or revelations—that had been entrusted specifically to the Jews.[11] This collection may have very well included the Gospel of Thomas, though the 13th Apostle does not say whether the collection was in book form or if it was merely oral tradition, or perhaps a mixture of both.

DATING THOMAS

Based on the papyri's orthography and use of the codex format (rather than, for instance, a scroll format), as well as the fact that the leaf fragments were discovered alongside documents that seem to have come from between the 2nd and 3rd Centuries, the Gospel of Thomas is conventionally viewed as having been written during that same particular period; namely, between the 2nd and 3rd Centuries—though some posit an even later date, as late as the 4th Century. A few Greek fragments of Thomas have been discovered that scholars date to around 200 A.D.[12] But since these are likely copies of earlier texts they do not help us establish when the original was written.

Most scholars maintain that Thomas could not have been written earlier than 100 A.D. and no later than 300 A.D., with an overall generally agreed upon date that places it in the early to mid 2nd Century.[13] The discoverers themselves, Grenfell and Hunt, reckoned that Thomas was written no later than 140 A.D.,[14] but admitted that it could have been created "earlier."[15] No less an authority than Robinson theorizes that our Gospel may date from "as early as the second half of the first century," which would place it between 50 and 99 A.D.[16] Patterson too gives Thomas a 1st-Century date; but again during the second half, in this case between 70 and 80 A.D.[17]

As I will justify shortly, however, I believe that Thomas was created in the *first half* of the 1st Century, which, if true, means that Grenfell and Hunt's Oxyrhynchus papyri are later copies, thoroughly reworked to fit the taste and style of Christian readers living 100 to 300 years later. This same Bible-translating custom continues today, which, tragically, in my opinion, has produced versions of the Old and New Testaments that would be utterly unrecognizable to those living in the 1st Millennium A.D.[18] This dangerous, destructive, Christianity-damaging practice was highlighted by Spiritualist Arthur Findlay, who uncovered some 36,191 mistranslations in the King James Version alone.[19]

GEOGRAPHICAL ORIGIN OF THOMAS
While the exact town or even region where the Gospel of Thomas was composed cannot now be known with any certainty, it is generally agreed that it was most likely written in the area the first fragments, and later the complete manuscript, were discovered; namely Egypt,[20] and more specifically Upper Egypt.

AUTHORSHIP OF THE GOSPEL OF THOMAS

Bust of St. Thomas, Ortona, Italy.

As its title clearly denotes, by tradition the work is ascribed to St. Thomas, a Jew living in the Middle East during the 1st Century A.D. Better known theologically as Didymos Judas Thomas,[21] he was one of the 12 Apostles and is best remembered as "doubting Thomas" in the famed story found in the canonical Gospel of John.[22]

St. Thomas' historical identity is quite confused, however, with theories ranging from him being Judas the son of James, or Jude the brother of Jesus, to him being an actual twin brother of Jesus—this theory due to the fact that both the names Thomas and Didymos translate as "twin."[23]

Interestingly, according to Eusebius, St. Thomas went to India after our Lord's death to preach and to establish Christian churches.[24] Evidence is seemingly plentiful.[25] This voyage may not have been accidental: St. Thomas could have been following in the Master's footsteps, for, according to many well-established early Asian traditions, Jesus Himself traveled throughout India during His "missing years," that is, between the ages of 12 and 30, to study, preach, and gain religious knowledge and spiritual insight. I believe this view has merit and I have written extensively on the topic.[26]

Whoever St. Thomas the man was, two points that nearly everyone seems to agree on regarding the Gospel of Thomas is that its author-editor was probably an Alexandrian Jewish-Christian[27] (that is, a "Jew who has heartily embraced Christianity"),[28] and that his true identity will forever remain unknown. As this Apostle was "notably popular" in the first few centuries A.D.,[29] we cannot totally rule out a connection between St. Thomas and our gospel. Yet, the attachment of his personal name to the Gospel of Thomas is generally considered a "bold invention of the editor."[30]

Lastly, it should be pointed out that the anonymous author-editor and his gospel have been associated—loosely or indirectly via the Nag Hammadi Library—with various early Jewish, Gnostic, and Jewish-Christian groups, including the Essenes,[31] the Docetics,[32] the Naassenes,[33] the Ebionites,[34] the Sethites,[35] the Manichaeans,[36] the Valentinians,[37] and the Therapeutae.[38] Although, note that it is not always clear if the Victorian scholars and early 20th-Century writers discussing "Thomas" are referring to the unconnected Infancy Gospel of Thomas, originally entitled the "Gospel of Thomas" (and possibly written in the mid 2nd Century A.D., and with dozens of different manuscript versions extant), or the topic of this book, the actual Gospel of Thomas (which I believe may have been written during Jesus' lifetime).[39]

To add more disorder to the situation, there are numerous other works associated with St. Thomas, such as the Gospel of Thomas the Israelite,[40] the Acts of Thomas, the Book of Thomas the Contender,[41] the Revelation of Thomas, and the Books of Thomas,[42] to name but a few; and in his infamous anti-Gnostic tome *Refutation of All Heresies*, (or *Philosophoumena*), Hippolytus mentions a "Gospel of Thomas" that may or may not be the same as the gospel that is the focus of this book.[43]

THOMAS AS A MYSTICAL WORK
Of course, the Gospel of Thomas having been discovered nearly a century ago, there has been plenty of time for speculation, the result being that today we have a wide spectrum of theories, views, and opinions in answer to the questions above. These range from the conservative, conventional, and orthodox to the mystical, "heretical," and purely scientific.

The Logia of Jesus, first series, verso. Dimensions: 3¾" wide, 5¾" high; discovered in 1897 at Oxyrhynchus, Egypt, by Grenfell and Hunt.

As a Christian mystic I will be found toward the left end of the scale, with my own views on Christianity, Jesus, and the origins of our religion being what most would consider nontraditional. As such, I fall in line with individuals like St. Paul, St. John the Apostle, Origen, St. Francis of Assisi, Catherine of Siena, St. Gregory of Nyssa, Meister Eckhart, Julian of Norwich, John of the Cross, Valentinus, and Hildegard of Bingen.[44]

Though my views on the Gospel of Thomas are to be found in the least popular category as defined by Christian scholars, the Christian clergy, and the Christian laity, I believe that they have just as much validity as the more traditionally accepted views, *if not more so*. For the writer (or writers) of the Gospel of Thomas was clearly a nontraditional Christian—in this case, a Middle Eastern mystic—and thus its profound spiritual message will be best ascertained through a Christian mystic's lens rather than through the cold calculating microscope of science or the highly subjective filter of conventional Christianity.

If more proof of the Gospel's mystical roots is needed we have only to look at the prologue that opens the first page: "These are the *secret* sayings that the living Jesus spoke." The word "secret" here is obviously meant to designate something arcane, cabalistic, or occultish. As even mainstream scholars and theologians admit that Thomas is acroamatic in nature,[45] there can be little doubt then that with this particular gospel we are entering into a world of magic, esoterica, and sibylline mysteries; in other words, Jewish-Christian mysticism—an overtly syncretistic theological system with roots firmly planted in the soil of Asian Paganism.

Since Jesus Himself was clearly a mystic, and since the entire Bible itself is obviously a mystical work, I feel I am on solid ground labeling the Gospel of Thomas a *thoroughly mystical document*.[46]

THE TRADITIONALLY ACCEPTED VIEW OF THOMAS

In large part the now widely accepted view of the Gospel of Thomas was laid out long ago, possibly as early as 1957. It goes something like this: A "late" fictitious work, Thomas was penned in the 2nd, 3rd, or even 4th Century, by a disgruntled radical Christian who purloined and rewrote the canonical teachings of Jesus (as found in the New Testament) in order to fit them into his own personal mystical framework; one intended for an elite audience of Christian intellectuals, insurgents, and disillusioned esoteric followers who misunderstood, or disagreed with, the doctrines of mainstream Christianity.[47]

As a derivative, post New Testament, and therefore "false," "deviant," "illegitimate," "foreign," "anti-evangelical representation,"[48] and "spurious and noxious Gospel"[49]—as its foes label it—the Gospel of Thomas therefore would be, and of course was, relegated to the trash bin of "invalid" Christian writings; nothing more than an "early perversion of Christianity,"[50] an apocryphal "Gnostic" treatise with allegedly no connection to the real Jesus or to authentic Christianity.[51] In this way, at least according to the mainstream Church and conventional Christian scholarship, the "idle tale" known as the Gospel of Thomas became an object of mere paleographic curiosity, a tiny, insignificant, and "shameful" footnote in the massive 2,000 year old record of the history of the Christian Church. The sooner it was pushed aside and forgotten the better.

Traditional Christian iconography.

As an example of the orthodox Christian position on, not just Thomas, but *all* of the apocryphal gospels, we have only to quote English scholar Benjamin Harris Cowper, who, in 1897, voiced his opinion on one of these entitled, the Infancy Gospel of Thomas (no currently known relation to our Gospel of Thomas):

> "[The Infancy Gospel of Thomas] may be viewed as a collection of foolish traditions, or fables invented to supply an account of that period in our Lord's history, respecting which the genuine Gospels are almost silent. These fables were probably varied and multiplied by the writer. The most noticeable features of the book are its grossly fictitious character, and its anti-evangelical representations; or, as

Bishop Ellicott says, 'pious fraud and disguised heresy.' It is of course utterly worthless, except as illustrating the recklessness of many professed followers of Christ at an early period."[52]

We might also quote William Greenough Thayer Shedd, who, in 1893, wrote of the apocryphal gospels in general:

> "These legendary and spurious narratives have never been regarded with respect or confidence even by the most credulous and superstitious portions of Christendom. The Papal church, though accepting the Old Testament Apocrypha, had too much sense and discrimination to place the Apocryphal Gospels in the canon. The consequence is, that these productions are about as unknown and obsolete a portion of literature as can be mentioned. No one has ever built a theory upon them; and no one has gone to them to derive either the doctrine or the person of Jesus Christ. They have died from utter contempt, and are as dead as a door-nail."[53]

By identifying the Infancy Gospel of Thomas, and by association all noncanonical gospels, as "grossly fictitious," "disguised heresy," a "collection of foolish traditions," and above all, "dead as a doornail," mainline Christianity has long hoped to render extra-New Testament works like Thomas harmless, turning them into meaningless ancient pablum that presents no danger to conventional Christian thought, belief, and doctrine.

THE LIVING WORDS OF THE LIVING JESUS

But as we shall see, the words of Jesus as found in Thomas, just as those found in the canonical Gospels, are living, ever-present, and immortal; for they are not concerned with any of the events that are alleged to have occurred between A.D. 1 and A.D. 33, or even Christianity itself. Rather they are cosmic ideas that are perpetually present in the eternal here and now; deep mystical concepts that are raceless, nationless, timeless, and above all religionless, delivering a message of hope and love designed to be heard by all people, at all times, of all backgrounds, and of all beliefs. These cosmic elements set the Gospel of Thomas outside both time and space, making it nearly impermeable to contemporary criticism.

THE MYSTICAL CHRISTIAN VIEW OF THOMAS

Still, the conventional largely negative view of the Gospel of Thomas continues to hold sway. But is Thomas' Gospel truly a heretical, "anti-evangelical" text, unfit for study or even consideration? Or is this only what limited-thinking Christian traditionalists insist it must be?

In my mystical Christian opinion the Gospel of Thomas is the opposite of what has been taught and accepted: It is a pre-Christian, pre-New Testament, pre-synoptic writing, some of which was later "borrowed" by the New Testament Gospelers, twisted and rephrased for an orthodox Christian audience, then inserted into the Bible canon as the divinely inspired words of Jesus and His companions.

I do not have proof for my view. However, there is currently no conclusive or consensual proof of *any* of the hundreds of theories about Thomas—in particular the traditionally recognized one. In fact, I closely associate Thomas with the Gospel of Q (as do a few others),[54] a work that I also believe to be pre-Christian, and another topic upon which I have written in detail.[55] This means that it is possible that both Thomas and Q derive from the same source: the absolute earliest, that is, the first, collection of Jesus's sayings—not preserved, of course, because it was oral in nature.

Jesus teaching the principles of, not the Kingdom of Jesus Christ, but the Kingdom of Heaven.

While I have nothing but the greatest respect for the laborious and detailed research scholars have put into the study of Thomas—and as a historian and scholar myself, I seriously consider their findings and expertise in my studies—in the end, as a Christian mystic I "walk by faith, not by sight."[56] For we cannot and will never know the full and complete truth behind the Gospel of Thomas (or even the New Testament, for that matter) anymore than we will ever know and understand

God, the infinite Creative Intelligence that produced and continues to rule the universe.⁵⁷

This does not mean, of course, that we should not try to understand the Gospel of Thomas. In fact, as Christians, whatever brand you hold yourself to be, it is our responsibility to try and decipher the lost ancient Christian texts that are occasionally uncovered in the parched scorching sands of the Middle East. For are they not shreds of evidence of the Divine placed at our disposal by God Himself, specifically designed for our spiritual edification? I believe so, and a close reading of the Gospel of Thomas itself suggests as much.

BACKGROUND OF THE GOSPEL OF THOMAS

On what do I base my view that Thomas is pre-Christian, a work that dates from the early 1ˢᵗ Century, long before the orthodox Christian religion was officialized in A.D. 380 by the Roman Emperor Theodosius?

As pointed out above, Thomas is essentially a work of mysticism, and more generally, Pagan-Jewish-Christian mysticism (in this case steeped in syncretistic Greek and Egyptian Gnostic flavorings)—a theology that mainstream Christians have always regarded as a form of unorthodox or heterodox Christianity.⁵⁸

The Pagan ankh, assimilated by the ancient Christian Church.

As possible evidence for my view let us take, for instance, one of the Nag Hammadi codices (the library in which the "complete" Gospel of Thomas was found): Codex II is embellished with a thoroughly heathen emblem: The ancient Egyptian ankh⁵⁹—a Pagan symbol of life that later became the Christian cross type known as the crux ansata.⁶⁰ Likewise, several scribal notes (in Codices III and IV) bear the emblem of a fish,⁶¹ a pre-Christian Pagan symbol connected to the ancient Egyptian Goddess Isis, a female deity associated with the fecundity of water.⁶² Additionally, the walls of caves located near to where the Nag Hammadi Library was

The Pagan fish symbol, adopted by ancient Christians.

discovered contained Greek prayers to the Pagan deity Zeus painted in red letters.[63] Zeus, of course, was one of the many pre-Christian father-gods later assimilated to the figure of the Jewish father-god Yahweh or Jehovah.[64]

Today's Christmas tree began in ancient times as the Pagan winter solstice tree, a symbol of immortality.

I am not saying that these facts prove that the Gospel of Thomas has Pagan roots; merely that the zeitgeist in which Thomas was created was one of profound non-Christian mysticism—which obviously deeply influenced it.

In my view, historically speaking, heterodoxy generally precedes orthodoxy, the latter tending to be a rearticulated conventionalized copy of the former, rather than the other way around, as traditional Christians continue to teach. An excellent example of this is the holy day we call Christmas, which was celebrated (though not by that name) around the world for thousands of years before Jesus' birth. The organized Church adopted the Pagan holy day (essentially a winter solstice celebration) and Christianized it, transforming it into the holiday we know today.[65]

I am supported in my view by the notable 3rd-Century Christian theologian and author Tertullian, who asserted:

> "That is the true faith which is most ancient, and that a corruption which is modern."[66]

This is why what we now call the "unorthodox" from among the early Christians (namely the ancient Gnostics and all of their associated contemporary groups), viewed themselves in their day as the one and only true "orthodox" Christians.[67] In one ancient Gnostic text, the Apocalypse of Peter, Jesus is shown calling orthodox Christians "blasphemers of the truth," "proclaimers of evil teachings," and the "messengers of error"[68]—the same view held by many nontraditional Christians to this day.

THE ORIGINAL CHRISTIANS
This being true, then the modern Christian Church is a late orthodox facsimile of the far earlier Gnostic Christian

Church—which, in reality, was not so much a formalized ecclesiastical institution, but rather a wide syncretistic assortment of esoteric Christian, Jewish-Christian, Hermetic Christian, Neoplatonic Christian, Essenic-like Christian, and Pagan-Christian sects holding a myriad of disparate belief systems that modern scholars have placed under the general heading "Gnosticism." Some have disparagingly referred to this movement as an "early Christian cult."[69] But nothing could be further from the truth, for Gnosticism *was* the original Christian religion.

Note that this would, of course, make conventional Christianity an "early Christian cult," the difference here being that this particular "cult" eventually grew (for a variety of reasons) into the all-powerful state religion of Rome, allowing it to violently stamp out its original opponent, Gnostic Christianity.

Evidence of these groups, the first Christians, could still be found during the life of St. Paul (who lived until A.D. 67, 34 years after Jesus' death), whose New Testament writings reveal some of the conflicts that arose between them as the beginnings of the modern conventional Christian Church began to take shape and Gnosticism was simultaneously being marginalized, copied, reinterpreted, and rewritten to fit the orthodox views of its new more mainstream leaders.[70] Gnostic leaders, like Simon Magus, Hymenaeus, and Philetus, along with gnosis itself (the secret "knowledge" of the Gnostics), were further demonized as what we now call established Christianity took control and began to formally organize the faith.[71] Ever since that time, Gnosticism has come to be seen as a late "rival" of orthodox Christianity,[72] rather than what I believe to be the case: orthodox Christianity was actually the late "rival" of Gnostic Christianity, which as noted, was the original "Church."

THOMAS: THE FIRST GOSPEL?
If we consider Thomas, or even parts of it, to be specifically Gnostic in origin, as many conventional scholars do,[73] we have even more proof, for Gnosticism has its roots in ancient Egypt, which began some 5,100 years ago, or 3,100 years before the birth of Jesus. As the concept of the Christ (or Christus) itself has its origins in ancient Egypt, it is obvious that the spiritual foundations of

Christianity are far older than the modern structured religion itself.[74] Furthering this idea, Grenfell and Hunt acknowledge that at least one of the sayings in Thomas "presents a very primitive kind of Gnosticism." They also note that there is "substantial evidence" that many of the sayings are cast from a pre-Resurrection point of view; that is, during Jesus' lifetime.[75] Both of these facts, in my opinion, offer further possible proof that Thomas was written in the first half of the 1st Century.

It is from out of this milieu that I believe the Gospel of Thomas, like the Gospel of Q, was written: either as a collection of Jesus' original oral sayings gathered and compiled shortly before or near the end of His life, between A.D. 28 and 33, or one put together shortly after His death, perhaps between A.D. 33 and 40. Let us note that the gospel's prologue makes reference to Jesus as "living" at the time the sayings were recorded and collected. Is this meant to be figurative or literal?

Fragments of ancient papyri.

In either case, these theories and facts place Thomas years, and in some cases decades, before the writing of even the earliest book in the New Testament: James, a Nazarean, anti-Pauline text probably penned around the year A.D. 50.[76]

ORAL TRADITION IN THE FIRST FOUR CENTURIES

Whatever the case turns out to be, pre-New Testament or post-New Testament, we know that Thomas was not copied from the Gospels. For surprisingly, though Thomas is synoptic rather than Johannine in tone (and has parallels only with Matthew and Luke),[77] there seems to be literally no direct connection between Thomas and any of the four canonical Gospels.[78] Writing in 1920, Evelyn-White, who believed that Thomas was authored in the 2nd or 3rd Century, could still assert that:

"In the first place we can say positively that the Sayings [of Thomas] are not extracts from the Canonical Gospels. Some of the Sayings are completely new; others, indeed, approach one or other of the Gospels very nearly at certain points, but with such differences as preclude not only the theory of direct extraction but even of loose citation."[79]

To set our topic in perspective, I believe that the Gospel of Mark was written as late as A.D. 90, the Gospel of Matthew was written as late as A.D. 95, the Gospel of John was written as late as A.D. 115, and the Gospel of Luke was written as late as A.D. 180. Since the four canonical Gospels are actually pseudonymous or pseudopigraphical works (based on astrology's four quarter signs, St. Irenaeus artificially named them in the year 180),[80] their true authors are unknown, making all four of even these dates highly speculative and debatable. All the same, if I am correct, this would naturally mean that the late canonical Gospelers copied from the earlier Gospel of Thomas rather than the other way around.

As nearly all (95 percent) of people living in the first few centuries A.D. only knew of Jesus through oral tradition,[81] let us note here that I am far from the only one who believes that both oral and written collections of Jesus sayings began to be compiled toward the end of his life, or shortly after it ended, or that these were used

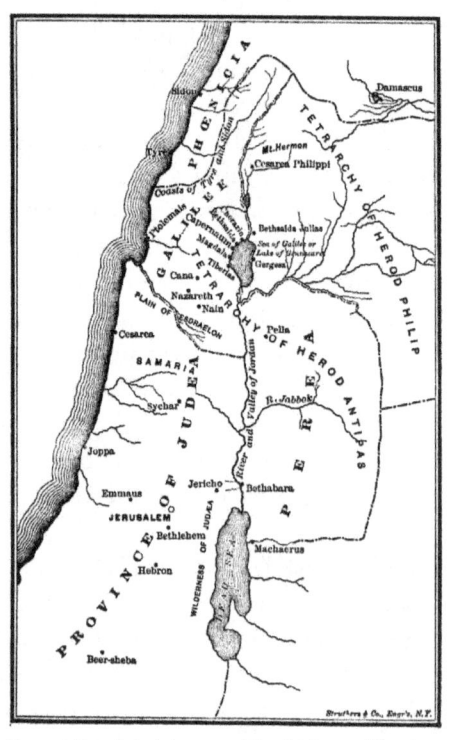

Conventional sketch map of the history of the four canonical Gospels.

by the editor (or editors) of the Gospel of Thomas in composing a loose list of our Lord's sayings. Among my fellow supporters have been such august scholars as Dr. Adolf von Harnack, Dr. Rendel Harris, and Professor Kirsopp Lake.[82] Some experts and academics go as far as to say that "probably many such collections were made,"[83] with the "scholarly consensus" being that an "original" gospel upon which all others are derived was written in Greek in Syria.[84]

The Logia of Jesus, second series, discovered in 1903 at Oxyrhynchus, Egypt, by Grenfell and Hunt.

Let us also consider the following: St. Paul references an agraphon in the Book of Acts, citing a statement by Jesus that is found nowhere else.[85] Acts was written (according to tradition, by Luke) as early as the year A.D. 60. Where did Paul find this quote if not in an already existing sayings collection? Clement of Rome is known to have cited agrapha as well,[86] while both Matthew and Mark give evidence that they depended on a "primitive collection" of Jesus' aphorisms (now known as the Gospel of Q).[87] Clearly not everything Jesus said and did is recorded in the New Testament, as even St. John the Gospeler himself admits.[88]

To be clear, I am not necessarily claiming that Thomas itself, as it now stands, was written in the first half of the 1st Century. Rather I am saying that the current Gospel of Thomas is almost certainly an edited, improved, and modernized copy of oral and perhaps written sayings of the "living Jesus" that date from just before His death. The original discoverers of the Oxyrhynchus papyri, Grenfell and Hunt, admit that

> "the Sayings themselves can and do contain . . . some elements which are not derived from the Canonical Gospels, and [which] go back to the first century."[89]

WHO COMPILED THE GOSPEL OF THOMAS?

The title claims that the Apostle Thomas is the compiler-editor (Taylor refers to him as the "Logiographer"),[90] as well as the speaker, of the Gospel of Thomas. Based on the centuries of scholarship behind early Christian literature, however, this assertion is to be far more doubted than readily accepted. In fact, the work, like the four canonical Gospels, is widely assumed to be pseudopigraphical, the title of an Apostle being falsely assigned to it to lend it both credibility and an air of authenticity.[91] Evelyn-White states the matter this way:

> ". . . if we judge the Sayings [i.e., the Gospel of Thomas]—as we must—by their Synoptic parallels, we must conclude that neither were they the fruit of private revelation, nor have they any connection with Thomas [the Apostle]."[92]

This being true, in my opinion a more objective and scholarly title for the Gospel of Thomas would have been: "The Jesus Oracles of Oxyrhynchus," or simply "The Oxyrhynchus Oracles."

AUDIENCE BEING ADDRESSED BY THE GOSPEL
As with many other aspects of Thomas, and indeed many early Christian writings in general, there is no definitive answer to this question. It is entirely unclear, for example, as to whether the speaker is addressing St. Thomas alone, St. Thomas and another Apostle, or possibly a group of Disciples that did not include St. Thomas.[93] For at times the speaker seems to be communicating with an audience that is neutral, at other times the sayings are spoken in the second person singular, and on at least one occasion his audience is addressed in the plural. Was our gospel meant to be used solitarily and individually or publicly and liturgically? Taylor writes:

> ". . . the logiographer has detached the sayings of the Lord from their settings in some form of the Gospel narrative, and has introduced them abruptly in his booklet with the words, 'Saith Jesus.' Thus . . . as Professor Harnack remarks, [there is generally] 'no indication of the occasion; this cannot be primary; the compiler was concerned only with the Saying, and he left out the occasion.'"[94]

Thus, it is almost universally accepted that the text is not original (to the author-editor), but was extracted from other documents (that is, it was not independent), and that therefore the Gospel of Thomas itself is not genuine—that is, it is not an original work of the author-editor.[95]

EARLY EVIDENCE FOR THOMAS
Despite the many questions we have about the Gospel of Thomas, we can be certain of the following: Like the Gospel of Q, it was a real document, one that was both cherished by members of the ancient Jesus movement and one that was circulated among the primitive Christian communities of the first three or four centuries—particularly "in the chief towns of Upper Egypt" where it was discovered, and where, apparently, it was both read "and presumably accepted as genuine."[96]

Jesus blessing the little children.

As proof we have a host of ancient individuals who claim to be eyewitnesses of, or at least earwitnesses to, the Gospel of Thomas. For instance, there was: Origen, Irenaeus, Eusebius, Bede, Hippolytus, Timothy of Constantinople, Pseudo-Photius, Didymus the Blind, Thomas Aquinas, St. Ambrose, Clement of Alexandria, Peter of Sicily, St. Jerome, Paul the Deacon, John of Damascus, Basilica, Pseudo-Leontinu of Byzantium, Nicephorus, Philip of Side, St. Cyril of Jerusalem, and George the Sinner, among many others.[97] The Gospel of Thomas is also referenced in numerous ancient works as well, such as the Gelasian Decree.[98] Some individuals, like Papias, spoke of extracanonical works, literary collections that may have included the Gospel of Thomas.[99] Such sources leave no doubt as to our document's ancient authenticity.

Miracle of the loaves: Jesus feeding the 5,000.

As for more nebulous but intriguing sources let us turn to intracanonical material. To start with, we have the Gospelers John and Luke, both who mention other Jesus biographers—though not by name.[100] In several places Mark suggests the existence of a collection of Jesus' sayings,[101] while in chapters five through seven, Matthew records the famous Sermon on the Mount, an event that the anonymous writer never witnessed in person.[102]

Let us go one step further: Where did Matthew, Mark, Luke and John get the copious Jesuine biographical material they used to write their gospels, if not for a variety of preexisting, pre-Gospel sayings collections? In his fourth chapter, Mark, for instance, lists a group of parables. Where did these come from? Mark had not written his Gospel yet. The same could be said for the other three gospelers, all of whom cite countless details about Jesus' life that they could not have known from firsthand experience.[103]

Naturally Paul too makes references to what seem to be a myriad of pre-Gospel collections of the words and deeds of Jesus; though again, the New Testament writers not being historians, including Paul, they go unnamed.[104] Since Paul was not an eyewitness to the real historical Jesus (his mystical conversion on the road to Damascus did not take place until several years after our Lord passed away), and since the four canonical Gospels had not yet been written, where did Paul receive his information about Jesus if not from a series of sayings collections that were then in circulation?[105]

It is my belief that one of these could very likely have been the Gospel of Thomas, which, as noted, may have been written as early as A.D. 28. Yet, the earliest of Paul's letters, 1 and 2 Thessalonians, were not penned until about A.D. 52. Again, the earliest Gospel, Mark's, was not authored until as late as the year A.D. 90. What pre-Gospel sources was Paul relying on to write his letters?

Lastly, all four canonical Gospels portray Jesus quite differently while contradicting one another on numerous occasions—more evidence that "Matthew," "Mark," "Luke," and "John" did not write their biographies from the point of view of actual eyewitnesses. Rather, it seems clear that they gathered their information from a number of miscellaneous sources; namely, portable, well-used compendiums of the traditional acts and words of Jesus already in existence. One of these could have been, and probably was, the Gospel of Thomas. If correct, some of Thomas' words, phrases, and ideas were then later copied and edited by the Synoptic Gospelers, as I have postulated.

Whatever the facts turn out to be, we can be sure that the Gospel of Thomas not only includes some of Jesus' actual words, but that it almost certainly existed prior to the New Testament. More evidence for this hypothesis comes from the fact that, as just one example, Thomas's version of the Parable of the Sower includes a particular detail missing from Matthew, Mark, and Luke's versions,[106] strongly suggesting that the parable, if not the Gospel of Thomas itself, existed prior, perhaps long prior, to the writing of the four canonical Gospels.[107]

THE JESUS OF THE GOSPEL OF THOMAS

Before moving on to the actual text of the Gospel itself, let us set aside, for the moment, our personal views of Jesus and his relationship to Christianity, whatever those may be. Instead, let us focus in on what I consider to be the most historically valuable element of Thomas; namely, the manner in which our Lord is portrayed.

There can be little doubt that some if not many of the quotations in Thomas came straight from the heart, mind, and lips of Jesus. However, unlike the Jesus of the four heavily redacted and reworked canonical Gospels, the Jesus of Thomas makes no claim to be either the messianic "only begotten son of God" or the founder of a new religion—a view that perfectly coincides with the New Testament, for here Jesus never once asserts that He is the "Son of God."[108] Instead, He represents Himself as a cosmic metaphysical preacher, a nontraditional spiritual guide, a New Thought teacher of deeply esoteric even Gnostic principles that have little or no connection to mainstream Judaism or even mainstream Christianity—the religion that was founded in His name in A.D. 313, *centuries after His death.*

This, after all, is very likely the primary reason the original three pages discovered by Grenfell and Hunt ended up in a rubbish mound at Oxyrhynchus: The book did not fit the "Messiah" narrative as laid out by Irenaeus and the Ecclesia, the organized orthodox Church—later fully established and sanctioned by Constantine the Great and the Council of Nicaea in May and June A.D. 325. For this it was literally torn up, shredded, burned, and trashed, and ultimately suppressed by conventional Christians. So thorough, sweeping, and

Jesus as the Good Shepherd, another Pagan motif borrowed by the early Christian Church.

insidious was this anti-Gnostic campaign that a full copy of the document was not discovered again until nearly 17 centuries later—an archaeological miracle if ever there was one.

Contrary to the modern mainstream—many would say, entirely corrupted and distorted—concept of Jesus, the Jesus of the Gospel of Thomas perfectly aligns with how the people of His time perceived Him: not as a supernatural god-man or "Savior of all mankind," but an ordinary human male, a wandering mystical Jewish mendicant who possessed phenomenal even radical spiritual insights into the nature of life, humanity, and God. In this way, like the early layers of the Gospel of Q, Jesus' sayings in the Gospel of Thomas are similar to the Zen Buddhist koan, a teaching methodology our Lord no doubt picked up during His sojourn into the Far East during His "lost years"[109]—the same time and place during which he learned the Sanskrit word yoga ("yoke").[110]

What is a koan?

Often used by Zen Buddhist masters on their students, it is a short, blunt, and seemingly irrational or oppositional statement, question, or parable, that is meant to jolt or shock the listener out of his or her rational state of mind. Its ultimate purpose is to push one into a different state of reality where the mind is more amenable to new, usually more cosmic, open-ended ways of thinking.

If one disregards for a moment what they learned in Sunday school and reads the New Testament slowly and meticulously, he or she will discover a host of references to Jesus, not as the "Supreme Eternal God, the maker of heaven and earth, and of all things visible and invisible,"[111] but simply as a "man"; a great teacher, healer, philosopher, and prophet yes—but still a man.

Numerous biblical references to Jesus as a mortal human being confirm this, as we shall now see. (I have italicized the relevant text in the following examples.) For instance, after one of Jesus' sermons to the masses, one individual in the crowd turned to the others and said:

> "Is not this *the carpenter's son*? Is not *his mother called Mary*? and *his brethren, James, and Joses, and Simon, and Judas*?"[112]

In the Gospel of Luke we read:

"Now *his parents* went to Jerusalem every year at the feast of the passover."[113]

After the boy Jesus gave an astonishingly mature sermon at the Temple, we read:

"And when they saw him, they were amazed: and *his mother* said unto him, 'Son, why hast thou thus dealt with us? behold, *thy father* and I have sought thee sorrowing.'"[114]

Luke gives Jesus' genealogy thusly:

And Jesus himself began to be about thirty years of age, being (as was supposed) *the son of Joseph*, which was the son of Heli . . ."[115]

After preaching at the synagogue in Nazareth, one of the members of His audience says to the others:

"Is not this *Joseph's son?*"[116]

While passing through the region of Galilee, Philip says to Nathanael:

"We have found him, of whom Moses in the law, and the prophets, did write, Jesus of Nazareth, *the son of Joseph*."[117]

After His sermon in Capernaum, the crowds muttered:

"Is not this Jesus, *the son of Joseph, whose father and mother we know?* how is it then that he saith, I came down from heaven?"[118]

The unknown author of the Book of Hebrews writes:

"For *this man* was counted worthy of more glory than Moses, inasmuch as he who hath builded the house hath more honour than the house."[119]

Also in Hebrews:

"But *this man*, because he continueth ever, hath an unchangeable priesthood."[120]

Another passage from Hebrews:

"But *this man*, after he had offered one sacrifice for sins for ever, sat down on the right hand of God."[121]

That the Apostles themselves also saw Jesus, not as a god but as a mortal, is proven by Peter's statement:

"Ye men of Israel, hear these words; Jesus of Nazareth, *a man* approved of God among you by miracles and wonders and signs, which God did by him in the midst of you, as ye yourselves also know."[122]

Christian mystic St. Paul, like Peter a Jew, took a similar stance, going as far as to carefully distinguish the man Jesus from the supernatural being God:

"For there is one God, and one mediator between God and men, *the man* Christ Jesus."[123]

Mainstream Jews, indeed, have viewed Jesus as a human being for 2,000 years, and continue to do so to this day. On this topic, Priestley, writing in 1871, states:

"The Jews were taught by their prophets to expect a Messiah, who was to be descended from the tribe of Judah, and the family of David, a person in whom themselves and all the nations of the earth should be blessed; but none of their prophets gave them an idea of any other than a man like themselves in that illustrious character, and no other did they ever expect, or do they expect to this day.

"Jesus Christ, whose history answers to the description given of the Messiah by the prophets, made no other pretensions; referring all his extraordinary power to God, his Father, who, he expressly says, spake and acted by him, and who raised him from the dead: and it is most evident that the apostles, and all those who conversed with our Lord before and after his resurrection, considered him in no other light than simply as a man . . ."[124]

Did Jesus Himself consider Himself God? Not according to scripture.

On a close reading of the New Testament we find that Jesus was adamant about the fact that while being one with God spiritually (as we all are),[125] He and God were separate beings. He went much further, however, even insisting that *all* of His powers were derived from the Father, not He Himself, and that His entire mission on earth, even His teachings, all came from God. The following New Testament story is illustrative:

Jesus pulling faithless Peter from the sea.

> "Now about the midst of the feast Jesus went up into the temple, and taught. And the Jews marvelled, saying, 'How knoweth this man letters, having never learned?' Jesus answered them, and said, *'My doctrine is not mine, but his that sent me. If any man will do his will, he shall know of the doctrine, whether it be of God, or whether I speak of myself. He that speaketh of himself seeketh his own glory: but he that seeketh his glory that sent him, the same is true, and no unrighteousness is in him.* . . . Then cried Jesus in the temple as he taught, saying, 'Ye both know me, and ye know whence I am: and *I am not come of myself*, but he that sent me is true, whom ye know not. But I know him: for I am from him, and he hath sent me.'"

Furthermore, we find Jesus constantly deflecting attention away from Himself, always redirecting it back onto God. "I seek not mine own glory," He repeatedly asserted.[126] When someone addressed Him as "good master," Jesus replied sharply: "Why callest thou me good? there is none good but one, that is, God."[127]

Many famous early Christians, such as Theodotus,[128] as well as may notable Christian groups, sects, and cults also rejected the idea that Jesus was a divinity, seeing him instead, as nearly everyone else did during this period, as a normal everyday man—though possessing spectacular teaching and healing powers. Among these were many members of, for example, the Nazarenes, the Docetics, the Ebionites, the Alogi, and of course Jewish Christians.[129]

For those still doubting we have the words of Jesus Himself. Was He truly the only human being capable of divine acts? Not according to the Master:

> "Verily, verily, I say unto you, *he that believeth on me, the works that I do shall he do also; and greater works than these shall he do*; because I go unto my Father."[130]

THE PAGANIZATION OF JESUS

Enlightened individuals from time immemorial have considered the Romanesque apotheosis of Jesus as nothing less than part of a grand Paganization scheme initiated by the early Catholic Church to lure in, convert, and baptize Pagans. Its intention? A massive and concerted effort to quickly increase the membership of the new religion while simultaneously crushing the old one.

Sun worship in ancient Egypt.

This was accomplished, in great part, by Christianizing the God of the Pagan Stoics, that great fundamental Pagan principle known as the Logos ("the Word"),[131] and overlaying it on the character of Jesus[132]—proof for which is found in the first verse of the first chapter of the Gospel of John.[133]

Just as importantly, the Catholic Church absorbed the figure and mythology of the chief Pagan sun deity known across the Roman world as Mithras. This syncretistic, pre-Christian "son of God" (borrowed from Zoroastrianism, then Romanized to fit the Mediterranean region) was born of a virgin on December 25, died and rose from the dead at the spring equinox, and was "born again" each year at the winter solstice.

Mithras had 12 apostles, held mass and established a bread sacrament, healed the sick and cast out demons, was worshiped weekly on the sun's sacred day (Sunday), and held as his sacred symbol the holy cross. Before returning to heaven, Mithras promised eternal life to his followers, then died a sacrificial death

The Sun-god Helios in his chariot, one of the many Pagan "Son-gods" assimilated to the figure of Jesus.

for the benefit of humanity. He was buried in a rock tomb, rising from the grave in spring, a divine act overseen by the Pagan goddess of spring Eostre—whose name later became Christianized as "Easter."[134]

With the resistless Christianization of Europe, Mithras, along with his many mythic Pagan accouterments, was adopted by the Church and cleverly painted over the figure of our Lord. In this way the Old Testament's "Sun of Righteousness"[135] later became seen as a prophecy regarding the coming of Jesus, the new "Son of Righteousness," all of this a blasphemous act that would have both disappointed and angered the real Jesus.

Many of His modern followers have been agitated by the Paganization of our Lord as well. One of the enlightened individuals I referred to above was U.S. President Thomas Jefferson, who in a letter to John Adams dated April 11, 1823, wrote (italics are mine):

> "The truth is, that *the greatest enemies of the doctrines of Jesus are those, calling themselves the expositors of them, who have perverted them for the structure of a system of fancy absolutely incomprehensible, and without any foundation in his genuine words.* And the day will come, when the mystical generation of Jesus, by the Supreme Being as His Father, in the womb of a virgin, will be classed with the fable of the generation of Minerva in the brain of Jupiter. But we may hope that the dawn of reason, and freedom of thought in these United States, will do away [with] all this artificial scaffolding, and restore to us the primitive and genuine doctrines of this the most venerated reformer of human errors."[136]

Another, Transcendendalist philosopher Ralph Waldo Emerson, noted bitterly of the biblical biographies of Jesus:

"... what a distortion did his doctrine and memory suffer in the same, in the next, and the following ages."[137]

Ancient Egyptian tomb relief of the pre-Christian annunciation, conception, birth, and adoration of the Pagan "Divine Child" or "Son of God" Horus. This motif was common around the ancient world, with hundreds of pre-Christian "Christs" having been identified so far.

In 1887 Egyptologist Gerald Massey expressed his anger with the devious tactics of the early Christian church and its politically-motivated apotheosis of Jesus (italics are mine):

> "*It would take almost a life-time of original research to fathom or approximately gauge the depths of ignorance in which the beginnings of Historic Christianity lie sunken out of sight.* The current ignorance of those pre-Christian evidences that have been preserved by the petrifying past must be well-nigh invincible, when a man like Professor [Benjamin] Jowett could say, as if with the voice of superstition in its dotage, 'To us the preaching of the Gospel is a New Beginning, from which we date all things; beyond which we neither desire, nor are able, to inquire.'
>
> "It is the commonly accepted orthodox belief that Christianity originated with the life, miracles, sayings, and teachings; the birth, death, resurrection, and ascension of an historic Jesus the Christ at the commencement of our era, called Christian; whereas, the origins were manifold, but mostly concealed. It is impossible to determine anything fundamental by an appeal to the documents which, alone out of a hundred Gospels, were made Canonical. And when Eusebius recorded his memorable boast that he had virtually made 'all square' for the Christians, it was an ominous announcement of what had been done to keep out of sight *the mythical and mystical rootage of historic Christianity*. The Gnostics had been muzzled, and their extant evidences, as far as possible, masked.
>
> "He and his co-conspirators did their worst in destroying documents and effacing the tell-tale records of the past, to

prevent the future from learning what the bygone ages could have said directly for themselves. They made dumb all Pagan voices that would have cried aloud their testimony against the unparalleled imposture then being perfected in Rome. They had almost reduced the first four centuries to silence on all matters of the most vital importance for any proper understanding of the true origins of the Christian Superstition. The mythos having been at last published as a human history *everything else was suppressed or forced to support the fraud*. Christolatry is founded on the Christ, who is mythical in one phase and mystical in the other; Egyptian (and Gnostic) in both, but historical in neither. *The Christ was a type and a title that could not become a person. As such, the Christ of the Gnostics was the Horus continued from Egypt and Chaldea; and that which was original as mythos ages earlier cannot be also original as a later personal history. We who commence with our canonical Gospels are three or four centuries too late to learn anything fundamental concerning the real beginnings of Christianity*.

"You have only to turn to the second Book of Esdras to learn that *Jesus the Christ of our canonical history was both pre-historic and, pre-Christian*. This is one of the books of the *hidden wisdom* which have been rejected and set apart as the Apocrypha—considered to be spurious, because they are opposed to the received history; whereas, *they contain the secret Gnosis ['knowledge']* by which alone we can identify the genuine Scripture. In this book it is said, 'My son Jesus shall be revealed with those that are with him and they that remain shall rejoice within four hundred years; and after these years shall my son Christ die, and all men shall have life.' And this was to be even as it had been in the former judgments at the end of the particular cycles of time, and the renewal of the world, which was to occur according to date!

"Now, if an historic Jesus Christ of prophecy is to be found anywhere it is here,—foretold even as the prediction is supposed to have been fulfilled. Yet these books are not included among the canonical Scriptures, *because they prove too much*; because they are historical in the wrong sense,—i.e., they are not and could not be made humanly historical; their Jesus Christ is entirely mythical,—[He] is the Kronian Christ; and his future coming therein announced was only the subject of *astronomical* prophecy."[138]

Is the deification of the human named Jesus, the man His contemporaries looked upon as the "son of Joseph and Mary," nothing more than Christian idolatry? I will let the reader decide for him or herself as to the truth or falsehood of these matters.[139]

Today, though it has been thoroughly rejected and demonized as a "heresy" by the Christian orthodoxy, modern Gnostic Christians, Gnostic Jews, Spiritualists, and Unitarians, among numerous others, continue to reject the Paganization of Jesus while upholding the ancient traditional view of our Lord as a human "everyman" who served as an example of what humanity could achieve spiritually by following his simple guidelines and rules.[140] For this belief, one held by both the Apostles and Jesus' friends and neighbors, ancient Unitarians were labeled *idiotae*: "idiots."[141] Yet, Grenfell and Hunt, the two scholars who originally discovered the first fragments of Thomas, did not consider the text "heretical."[142]

Symbol of the Christian Sun of Righteousness.

THOMAS PRESERVES THE ORIGINAL AUTHENTIC JESUS

We can see then that the original, ancient, traditional view of Jesus as a ordinary mortal man rather than an unapproachable supernatural being is the one preserved in the Gospel of Thomas. Brimming with esoteric wisdom and pantheistic mysticism, and completely lacking the overt and often childish Pagan mythology of the four canonical Gospels, Thomas contains nothing about Jesus' miraculous virgin birth, the Annunciation, the Nativity, the Adoration, the Epiphany, the Flight into Egypt, His boyhood experience at the Jerusalem temple, His Baptism, the 12 Apostles, the Three Temptations, His miracles, his conflicts with organized Judaism, the Passion, the Transfiguration, the Betrayal, His crucifixion and death on the cross, His burial, the Resurrection, the Ascension,

Christian Cathedral, Cologne, Germany.

or even the Parousia. It is a perfect example of early pre-Christian thought: simple, clean, and pure, untainted by what would later become known as mainstream Christianity, a religion today comprised of overly complex, manmade rules and Pagan mythology-saturated doctrines. Orthodox Christianity, in fact, has become a religion built around the Paganized messenger (Jesus) rather than around His ecumenical message (Theosis).[143]

In short, what we have in the Gospel of Thomas are remnants of the authentic man named Jesus—more evidence pointing to this document's great antiquity, possibly dating back to the years shortly before or after the Master's death around A.D. 33.

Having, for our introductory purposes, thoroughly dissected the Gospel of Thomas, let us now proceed to the actual manuscript.

Thomas the Apostle, wanting proof of Jesus' resurrection, was invited to touch one of the Master's wounds. Only then did he believe, bringing the still popular phrase "doubting Thomas" into mainstream vocabulary.

Ancient Egyptian zodiacal chart. Early vegetation cults, upon which survival literally depended at the time, were designed around the changing seasons and the movements of the corresponding astrological signs across the heavens. At the cults' religious center was the sun, imaged as dying-and-rising son-god, child of Virgo (the "Virgin"). The sun's/son's annual death and rebirth heralded another year of bountiful crops. The ancient Christian Church assimilated this Pagan motif, and overlaid it upon the figure of the historical Jesus. This is why, to this day, the birth (summer solstice), life (fall equinox), death (winter solstice), and resurrection (spring equinox) of Jesus can be both astronomically (literally) and astrologically (mystically) traced in Pagan diagrams of the constellations, like this one.

CHAPTER TWO

THE GOSPEL OF THOMAS

Original Text, 114 Jesus Sayings.
Compiled by "St. Thomas the Apostle."

Derived From Ancient Coptic Papyri.
Discovered by Two Egyptian Peasants
Near Nag Hammadi, Egypt, in 1945.

TRANSLATED BY MEMBERS OF THE
COPTIC GNOSTIC LIBRARY PROJECT
INSTITUTE FOR ANTIQUITY & CHRISTIANITY

SYMBOLS KEY
• Lacunae and estimations (gaps in the text): [ ]
• Editorial insertions: ( )
• Editorial corrections of scribal errors: / \

THE GOSPEL OF THOMAS

These are the secret sayings that the living Jesus spoke and Didymos Judas Thomas wrote down.

1: And he said, "Whoever discovers the meaning of these sayings won't taste death."

2: Jesus said, "Whoever seeks shouldn't stop until they find. When they find, they'll be disturbed. When they're disturbed, they'll be […] amazed, and reign over the All."

3: Jesus said, "If your leaders tell you, 'Look, the kingdom is in heaven,' then the birds of heaven will precede you. If they tell you, 'It's in the sea,' then the fish will precede you. Rather, the kingdom is within you and outside of you.

"When you know yourselves, then you'll be known, and you'll realize that you're the children of the living Father. But if you don't know yourselves, then you live in poverty, and you are the poverty."

4: Jesus said, "The older person won't hesitate to ask a little seven-day-old child about the place of life, and they'll live, because many who are first will be last, and they'll become one."

5: Jesus said, "Know what's in front of your face, and what's hidden from you will be revealed to you, because there's nothing hidden that won't be revealed."

6: His disciples said to him, "Do you want us to fast? And how should we pray? Should we make donations? And what food should we avoid?"

Jesus said, "Don't lie, and don't do what you hate, because everything is revealed in the sight of heaven; for there's nothing hidden that won't be revealed, and nothing covered up that will stay secret."

7: Jesus said, "Blessed is the lion that's eaten by a human and then becomes human, but how awful for the human who's eaten by a lion, and the lion becomes human."

8: He said, "The human being is like a wise fisher who cast a net into the sea and drew it up from the sea full of little fish. Among them the wise fisher found a fine large fish and cast all the little fish back down into the sea, easily choosing the large fish. Anyone who has ears to hear should hear!"

9: Jesus said, "Look, a sower went out, took a handful of seeds, and scattered them. Some fell on the roadside; the birds came and gathered them. Others fell on the rock; they didn't take root in the soil and ears of grain didn't rise toward heaven. Yet others fell on thorns; they choked the seeds and worms ate them. Finally, others fell on good soil; it produced fruit up toward heaven, some sixty times as much and some a hundred and twenty."

10: Jesus said, "I've cast fire on the world, and look, I'm watching over it until it blazes."

11: Jesus said, "This heaven will disappear, and the one above it will disappear too. Those who are dead aren't alive, and those who are living won't die. In the days when you ate what was dead, you made it alive. When you're in the light, what will you do? On the day when you were one, you became divided. But when you become divided, what will you do?"

12: The disciples said to Jesus, "We know you're going to leave us. Who will lead us then?"
    Jesus said to them, "Wherever you are, you'll go to James the Just, for whom heaven and earth came into being."

13: Jesus said to his disciples, "If you were to compare me to someone, who would you say I'm like?"
    Simon Peter said to him, "You're like a just angel."

Matthew said to him, "You're like a wise philosopher."

Thomas said to him, "Teacher, I'm completely unable to say whom you're like."

Jesus said, "I'm not your teacher. Because you've drunk, you've become intoxicated by the bubbling spring I've measured out."

He took him aside and told him three things. When Thomas returned to his companions, they asked, "What did Jesus say to you?"

Thomas said to them, "If I tell you one of the things he said to me, you'll pick up stones and cast them at me, and fire will come out of the stones and burn you up."

14: Jesus said to them, "If you fast, you'll bring guilt upon yourselves; and if you pray, you'll be condemned; and if you make donations, you'll harm your spirits.

"If they welcome you when you enter any land and go around in the countryside, heal those who are sick among them and eat whatever they give you, because it's not what goes into your mouth that will defile you. What comes out of your mouth is what will defile you.

15: Jesus said, "When you see the one who wasn't born of a woman, fall down on your face and worship that person. That's your Father."

16: Jesus said, "Maybe people think that I've come to cast peace on the world, and they don't know that I've come to cast divisions on the earth: fire, sword, and war. Where there are five in a house, there'll be three against two and two against three, father against and son and son against father. They'll stand up and be one."

17: Jesus said, "I'll give you what no eye has ever seen, no ear has ever heard, no hand has ever touched, and no human mind has ever thought."

18: The disciples said to Jesus, "Tell us about our end. How will it come?"

Jesus said, "Have you discovered the beginning so that you can look for the end? Because the end will be where the beginning is. Blessed is the one who will stand up in the beginning. They'll know the end, and won't taste death."

19: Jesus said, "Blessed is the one who came into being before coming into being. If you become my disciples and listen to my message, these stones will become your servants; because there are five trees in paradise which don't change in summer or winter, and their leaves don't fall. Whoever knows them won't taste death."

20: The disciples asked Jesus, "Tell us, what can the kingdom of heaven be compared to?"

He said to them, "It can be compared to a mustard seed. Though it's the smallest of all the seeds, when it falls on tilled soil it makes a plant so large that it shelters the birds of heaven."

21: Mary said to Jesus, "Whom are your disciples like?"

He said, "They're like little children living in a field which isn't theirs. When the owners of the field come, they'll say, 'Give our field back to us.' They'll strip naked in front of them to let them have it and give them their field.

"So I say that if the owner of the house realizes the bandit is coming, they'll watch out beforehand and won't let the bandit break into the house of their domain and steal their possessions. You, then, watch out for the world! Prepare to defend yourself so that the bandits don't attack you, because what you're expecting will come. May there be a wise person among you!

"When the fruit ripened, the reaper came quickly, sickle in hand, and harvested it. Anyone who has ears to hear should hear!"

22: Jesus saw some little children nursing. He said to his disciples, "These nursing children can be compared to those who enter the kingdom."

They said to him, "Then we'll enter the kingdom as little children?"

Jesus said to them, "When you make the two into one, and make the inner like the outer and the outer like the inner, and the upper like the lower, and so make the male and the female a single one so that the male won't be male nor the female female; when you make eyes in the place of an eye, a hand in the place of a hand, a foot in the place of a foot, and an image in the place of an image; then you'll enter [the kingdom]."

23: Jesus said, "I'll choose you, one out of a thousand and two out of ten thousand, and they'll stand as a single one."

24: His disciples said, "Show us the place where you are, because we need to look for it."
   He said to them, "Anyone who has ears to hear should hear! Light exists within a person of light, and they light up the whole world. If they don't shine, there's darkness."

25: Jesus said, "Love your brother as your own soul. Protect them like the pupil of your eye."

26: Jesus said, "You see the speck that's in your brother's eye, but you don't see the beam in your own eye. When you get the beam out of your own eye, then you'll be able to see clearly to get the speck out of your brother's eye."

27: "If you don't fast from the world, you won't find the kingdom. If you don't make the Sabbath into a Sabbath, you won't see the Father."

28: Jesus said, "I stood in the middle of the world and appeared to them in the flesh. I found them all drunk; I didn't find any of them thirsty. My soul ached for the children of humanity, because they were blind in their hearts and couldn't see. They came into the world empty and plan on leaving the world empty. Meanwhile, they're drunk. When they shake off their wine, then they'll change."

29: Jesus said, "If the flesh came into existence because of spirit, that's amazing. If spirit came into existence because of the body, that's really amazing! But I'm amazed at how [such] great wealth has been placed in this poverty."

30: Jesus said, "Where there are three deities, they're divine. Where there are two or one, I'm with them."

31: Jesus said, "No prophet is welcome in their own village. No doctor heals those who know them."

32: Jesus said, "A city built and fortified on a high mountain can't fall, nor can it be hidden."

33: Jesus said, "What you hear with one ear, listen to with both, then proclaim from your rooftops. No one lights a lamp and puts it under a basket or in a hidden place. Rather, they put it on the stand so that everyone who comes and goes can see its light."

34: Jesus said, "If someone who's blind leads someone else who's blind, both of them fall into a pit."

35: Jesus said, "No one can break into the house of the strong and take it by force without tying the hands of the strong. Then they can loot the house."

36: Jesus said, "Don't be anxious from morning to evening or from evening to morning about what you'll wear."

37: His disciples said, "When will you appear to us? When will we see you?"
   Jesus said, "When you strip naked without being ashamed, and throw your clothes on the ground and stomp on them as little children would, then [you'll] see the Son of the Living One and won't be afraid."

38: Jesus said, "Often you've wanted to hear this message that I'm telling you, and you don't have anyone else from whom to hear it. There will be days when you'll look for me, but you won't be able to find me."

39: Jesus said, "The Pharisees and the scholars have taken the keys of knowledge and hidden them. They haven't entered, and haven't let others enter who wanted to. So be wise as serpents and innocent as doves."

40: Jesus said, "A grapevine has been planted outside of the Father. Since it's malnourished, it'll be pulled up by its root and destroyed."

41: Jesus said, "Whoever has something in hand will be given more, but whoever doesn't have anything will lose even what little they do have."

42: Jesus said, "Become passersby."

43: His disciples said to him, "Who are you to say these things to us?"

"You don't realize who I am from what I say to you, but you've become like those Judeans who either love the tree but hate its fruit, or love the fruit but hate the tree."

44: Jesus said, "Whoever blasphemes the Father will be forgiven, and whoever blasphemes the Son will be forgiven, but whoever blasphemes the Holy Spirit will not be forgiven, neither on earth nor in heaven."

45: Jesus said, "Grapes aren't harvested from thorns, nor are figs gathered from thistles, because they don't produce fruit. [A person who's good] brings good things out of their treasure, and a person who's [evil] brings evil things out of their evil treasure. They say evil things because their heart is full of evil."

46: Jesus said, "From Adam to John the Baptizer, no one's been born who's so much greater than John the Baptizer that they shouldn't avert their eyes. But I say that whoever among you will become a little child will know the kingdom and become greater than John."

47: Jesus said, "It's not possible for anyone to mount two horses or stretch two bows, and it's not possible for a servant to follow two leaders, because they'll respect one and despise the other.

"No one drinks old wine and immediately wants to drink new wine. And new wine isn't put in old wineskins, because they'd burst. Nor is old wine put in new wineskins, because it'd spoil.

"A new patch of cloth isn't sewn onto an old coat, because it'd tear apart."

48: Jesus said, "If two make peace with each other in a single house, they'll say to the mountain, 'Go away,' and it will."

49: Jesus said, "Blessed are those who are one — those who are chosen, because you'll find the kingdom. You've come from there and will return there."

50: Jesus said, "If they ask you, 'Where do you come from?' tell them, 'We've come from the light, the place where light came into being by itself, [established] itself, and appeared in their image.'

"If they ask you, 'Is it you?' then say, 'We are its children, and we're chosen by our living Father.'

"If they ask you, 'What's the sign of your Father in you?' then say, 'It's movement and rest.'"

51: His disciples said to him, "When will the dead have rest, and when will the new world come?"

He said to them, "What you're looking for has already come, but you don't know it."

52: His disciples said to him, "Twenty-four prophets have spoken in Israel, and they all spoke of you."

He said to them, "You've ignored the Living One right in front of you, and you've talked about those who are dead."

53: His disciples said to him, "Is circumcision useful, or not?"

He said to them, "If it were useful, parents would have children who are born circumcised. But the true circumcision in spirit has become profitable in every way."

54: Jesus said, "Blessed are those who are poor, for yours is the kingdom of heaven."

55: Jesus said, "Whoever doesn't hate their father and mother can't become my disciple, and whoever doesn't hate their brothers and sisters and take up their cross like I do isn't worthy of me."

56: Jesus said, "Whoever has known the world has found a corpse. Whoever has found a corpse, of them the world isn't worthy."

57: Jesus said, "My Fathers' kingdom can be compared to someone who had [good] seed. Their enemy came by night and sowed weeds among the good seed. The person didn't let anyone pull out the weeds, 'so that you don't pull out the wheat along with the weeds,' they said to them. 'On the day of the harvest, the weeds will be obvious. Then they'll be pulled out and burned.'"

58: Jesus said, "Blessed is the person who's gone to a lot of trouble. They've found life."

59: Jesus said, "Look for the Living One while you're still alive. If you die and then try to look for him, you won't be able to."

60: They saw a Samaritan carrying a lamb to Judea. He said to his disciples, "What do you think he's going to do with that lamb?"
They said to him, "He's going to kill it and eat it."
He said to them, "While it's living, he won't eat it, but only after he kills it and it becomes a corpse."
They said, "He can't do it any other way."
He said to them, "You, too, look for a resting place, so that you won't become a corpse and be eaten."

61: Jesus said, "Two will rest on a couch. One will die, the other will live."
Salome said, "Who are you, Sir, to climb onto my couch and eat off my table as if you're from someone?"
Jesus said to her, "I'm the one who exists in equality. Some of what belongs to my Father was given to me."
"I'm your disciple."

"So I'm telling you, if someone is /equal\, they'll be full of light; but if they're divided, they'll be full of darkness."

62: Jesus said, "I tell my mysteries to [those who are worthy of my] mysteries. Don't let your left hand know what your right hand is doing."

63: Jesus said, "There was a rich man who had much money. He said, 'I'll use my money to sow, reap, plant, and fill my barns with fruit, so that I won't need anything.' That's what he was thinking to himself, but he died that very night. Anyone who has ears to hear should hear!"

64: Jesus said, "Someone was planning on having guests. When dinner was ready, they sent their servant to call the visitors.
 "The servant went to the first and said, 'My master invites you.'
 "They said, 'Some merchants owe me money. They're coming tonight. I need to go and give them instructions. Excuse me from the dinner.'
 "The servant went to another one and said, 'My master invites you.'
 "They said, "I've just bought a house and am needed for the day. I won't have time.'
 "The servant went to another one and said, 'My master invites you.'
 "They said, 'My friend is getting married and I'm going to make dinner. I can't come. Excuse me from the dinner.'
 "The servant went to another one and said, 'My master invites you.'
 "They said, "I've just bought a farm and am going to collect the rent. I can't come. Excuse me.'
 "The servant went back and told the master, 'The ones you've invited to the dinner have excused themselves.'
 "The master said to their servant, 'Go out to the roads and bring whomever you find so that they can have dinner.'
 "Buyers and merchants won't [enter] the places of my Father."

65: He said, "A [creditor] owned a vineyard. He leased it out to some sharecroppers to work it so he could collect its fruit.

"He sent his servant so that the sharecroppers could give him the fruit of the vineyard. They seized his servant, beat him, and nearly killed him.

"The servant went back and told his master. His master said, 'Maybe he just didn't know them.' He sent another servant, but the tenants beat that one too.

"Then the master sent his son, thinking, 'Maybe they'll show some respect to my son.'

"Because they knew that he was the heir of the vineyard, the sharecroppers seized and killed him. Anyone who has ears to hear should hear!"

66: Jesus said, "Show me the stone the builders rejected; that's the cornerstone."

67: Jesus said, "Whoever knows everything, but is personally lacking, lacks everything."

68: Jesus said, "Blessed are you when you're hated and persecuted, and no place will be found where you've been persecuted."

69: Jesus said, "Blessed are those who've been persecuted in their own hearts. They've truly known the Father. Blessed are those who are hungry, so that their stomachs may be filled."

70: Jesus said, "If you give birth to what's within you, what you have within you will save you. If you don't have that within [you], what you don't have within you [will] kill you."

71: Jesus said, "I'll destroy [this] house, and no one will be able to build it [...]"

72: [Someone said to him], "Tell my brothers to divide our inheritance with me."

He said to him, "Who made me a divider?"

He turned to his disciples and said to them, "Am I really a divider?"

73: Jesus said, "The harvest really is plentiful, but the workers are few. So pray that the Lord will send workers to the harvest."

74: He said, "Lord, many are gathered around the well, but there's nothing to drink."

75: Jesus said, "Many are waiting at the door, but those who are one will enter the bridal chamber."

76: Jesus said, "The Father's kingdom can be compared to a merchant with merchandise who found a pearl. The merchant was wise; they sold their merchandise and bought that single pearl for themselves.

"You, too, look for the treasure that doesn't perish but endures, where no moths come to eat and no worms destroy."

77: Jesus said, "I'm the light that's over all. I am the All. The All has come from me and unfolds toward me.

"Split a log; I'm there. Lift the stone, and you'll find me there."

78: Jesus said, "What did you go out into the desert to see? A reed shaken by the wind? A [person] wearing fancy clothes, [like your] rulers and powerful people? They (wear) fancy [clothes], but can't know the truth."

79: A woman in the crowd said to him, "Blessed is the womb that bore you, and the breasts that nourished you."

He said to [her], "Blessed are those who have listened to the message of the Father and kept it, because there will be days when you'll say, 'Blessed is the womb that didn't conceive and the breasts that haven't given milk.'"

80: Jesus said, "Whoever has known the world has found the body; but whoever has found the body, of them the world isn't worthy."

81: Jesus said, "Whoever has become rich should become a ruler, and whoever has power should renounce it."

82: Jesus said, "Whoever is near me is near the fire, and whoever is far from me is far from the kingdom."

83: Jesus said, "Images are revealed to people, but the light within them is hidden in the image of the Father's light. He'll be revealed, but his image will be hidden by his light."

84: Jesus said, "When you see your likeness, you rejoice. But when you see your images that came into being before you did – which don't die, and aren't revealed – how much you'll have to bear!"

85: Jesus said, "Adam came into being from a great power and great wealth, but he didn't become worthy of you. If he had been worthy, [he wouldn't have tasted] death."

86: Jesus said, "[The foxes have dens] and the birds have nests, but the Son of Humanity has nowhere to lay his head and rest."

87: Jesus said, "How miserable is the body that depends on a body, and how miserable is the soul that depends on both."

88: Jesus said, "The angels and the prophets will come to you and give you what belongs to you. You'll give them what you have and ask yourselves, 'When will they come and take what is theirs?'"

89: Jesus said, "Why do you wash the outside of the cup? Don't you know that whoever created the inside created the outside too?"

90: Jesus said, "Come to me, because my yoke is easy and my requirements are light. You'll be refreshed."

91: They said to him, "Tell us who you are so that we may trust you."
    He said to them, "You read the face of the sky and the earth, but you don't know the one right in front of you, and you don't know how to read the present moment."

92: Jesus said, "Look and you'll find. I didn't answer your questions before. Now I want to give you answers, but you aren't looking for them."

93: "Don't give what's holy to the dogs, or else it might be thrown on the manure pile. Don't throw pearls to the pigs, or else they might [...]"

94: Jesus [said], "Whoever looks will find, [and whoever knocks], it will be opened for them."

95: [Jesus said], "If you have money, don't lend it at interest. Instead, give [it to] someone from whom you won't get it back."

96: Jesus [said], "The Father's kingdom can be compared to a woman who took a little yeast and [hid] it in flour. She made it into large loaves of bread. Anyone who has ears to hear should hear!"

97: Jesus said, "The Father's kingdom can be compared to a woman carrying a jar of flour. While she was walking down [a] long road, the jar's handle broke and the flour spilled out behind her on the road. She didn't know it, and didn't realize there was a problem until she got home, put down the jar, and found it empty."

98: Jesus said, "The Father's kingdom can be compared to a man who wanted to kill someone powerful. He drew his sword in his house and drove it into the wall to figure out whether his hand was strong enough. Then he killed the powerful one."

99: The disciples said to him, "Your brothers and mother are standing outside."
    He said to them, "The people here who do the will of my Father are my brothers and mother; they're the ones who will enter my Father's kingdom."

100: They showed Jesus a gold coin and said to him, "Those who belong to Caesar demand tribute from us."
    He said to them, "Give to Caesar what belongs to Caesar, give to God what belongs to God, and give to me what belongs to me."

101: "Whoever doesn't hate their [father] and mother as I do can't become my [disciple], and whoever [doesn't] love their [father] and mother as I do can't become my [disciple]. For my mother [...], but [my] true [Mother] gave me Life."

102: Jesus said, "How awful for the Pharisees who are like a dog sleeping in a feeding trough for cattle, because the dog doesn't eat, and [doesn't let] the cattle eat either."

103: Jesus said, "Blessed is the one who knows where the bandits are going to enter. [They can] get up to assemble their defenses and be prepared to defend themselves before they arrive."

104: They said to [Jesus], "Come, let's pray and fast today."
    Jesus said, "What have I done wrong? Have I failed?
    "Rather, when the groom leaves the bridal chamber, then people should fast and pray."

105: Jesus said, "Whoever knows their father and mother will be called a bastard."

106: Jesus said, "When you make the two into one, you'll become Children of Humanity, and if you say 'Mountain, go away!', it'll go."

107: Jesus said, "The kingdom can be compared to a shepherd who had a hundred sheep. The largest one strayed. He left the ninety-nine and looked for that one until he found it. Having gone through the trouble, he said to the sheep: 'I love you more than the ninety-nine.'"

108: Jesus said, "Whoever drinks from my mouth will become like me, and I myself will become like them; then, what's hidden will be revealed to them."

109: Jesus said, "The kingdom can be compared to someone who had a treasure [hidden] in their field. [They] didn't know about it. After they died, they left it to their son. The son didn't know it either. He took the field and sold it.

"The buyer plowed the field, [found] the treasure, and began to loan money at interest to whomever they wanted."

110: Jesus said, "Whoever has found the world and become rich should renounce the world."

111: Jesus said, "The heavens and the earth will roll up in front of you, and whoever lives from the Living One won't see death."

Doesn't Jesus say, "Whoever finds themselves, of them the world isn't worthy"?

112: Jesus said, "How awful for the flesh that depends on the soul. How awful for the soul that depends on the flesh."

113: His disciples said to him, "When will the kingdom come?"

"It won't come by looking for it. They won't say, 'Look over here!' or 'Look over there!' Rather, the Father's kingdom is already spread out over the earth, and people don't see it."

114: Simon Peter said to them, "Mary should leave us, because women aren't worthy of life."

Jesus said, "Look, am I to make her a man? So that she may become a living spirit too, she's equal to you men, because every woman who makes herself manly will enter the kingdom of heaven."

Jesus teaching at the Temple.

CHAPTER THREE

THE GOSPEL OF THOMAS

The Original Text, 114 Jesus Sayings,
With a 21st-Century Scripture-by-Scripture
Reinterpretation by Christian Mystic
Lochlainn Seabrook

INTRODUCTION

THE KEY THAT UNLOCKS the door to understanding the Gospel of Thomas is quite elementary: As previously discussed, in original Christianity Jesus was not seen as *the* Son of God. He was viewed, like everyone else was, as *a* son of God.[144] But not just an ordinary son of God. He was imaged as an extraordinary teacher, healer, philosopher, and prophet, one who personified Christ, and so was given that title.[145] As we have seen, Jesus Himself shunned the title "Son of God," instead always referring to Himself as the "Son of man,"[146] *Bar Nasha* being an ancient Aramaic term for an ordinary human being.[147]

What is Christ? It is a shortening of the mystical Christian term Christ Consciousness, an emancipating state of mind in which one discovers his or her own inner divinity, thereby experiencing unity with God, freeing one from the worries of daily life on the material plane.[148]

And here is a clue to the magic formula for reading and fully comprehending the Gospel of Thomas: Nothing should be or is meant to be read literally. Nearly all of it is, quite simply, symbolic and allegorical in nature. Thus, for instance, in Thomas, as in all esoteric works of this nature, "Jesus" is a symbol of Christ Consciousness (perfected in humanity), the "Kingdom of Heaven" is a symbol of being in a state of Christ Consciousness, the "Father" is a symbol of the unknowable Divine Creative Intelligence, the "Apostles" and "Disciples" are symbols of the spiritually unenlightened, "angels" are a symbol of our Higher Selves, "Satan" is a symbol of our Lower Selves, the Pharisees are a symbol of organized religion and mainstream thought, and so on.

This means that every time the word Jesus, or even the figure of Jesus, appears in a sentence, we will replace His personal name or appearance with the noun Christ (or, in some cases, depending on the nature of the saying, a related term). I am referring not to the man called Christ, but to the state of mind called Christ, which the canonical New Testament clearly shows is a separate entity from Jesus.[149]

Theologically, the concept of realizing one's oneness with the Divine is known as Theosis, meaning "God in Man." It is as old as humankind, for, in one form or another, this idea can be found in the sacred scriptures and spiritual teachings of every religion.[150] In the parlance of ancient times, St. Paul called Christ Consciousness the "mind of Christ"[151] or as being a "son of God,"[152] while Jesus Himself referred to it as entering the "Kingdom of God"[153] or the "Kingdom of Heaven."[154]

In Buddhism, Kingdom of God Consciousness or Christ Consciousness is known as Satori; in Hinduism it is called Moksha; in Judaism it is referred to as Kabbalah' in Jainism it is Samadhi; in Sikhism it is Nirvana; and in Sufism it is known as Tawhid. It is even found in nonreligious frameworks, such as psychology, where, for instance, Abraham Maslow used the term self-actualization and Carl Jung used the term individuation. Christ Consciousness is best known to both Christians and non-Christians, however, as enlightenment, while to ecumenical mystics it is called Cosmic Consciousness.[155] I have termed the attainment of this perfected state of mind self-Christhood.[156]

While I use the term Christ Consciousness in relation to this book due to the affiliation between the Gospel of Thomas and Christianity, as is obvious from the above, Christ Consciousness has no religious boundaries, and is not even specifically a religious doctrine. In fact, anyone can achieve Theosis, even an atheist. This is because realizing your oneness with the Universe has nothing to do with religion, but with psychology, a science that literally means the "study of the soul"—*the "soul" being an ancient euphemism for the mind.* For you are not your body or your brain. What existed before you were born was your mind, and what will live on after you leave earth is your mind, for that is the real you: You are your mind; or rather, you are mind.

To reemphasize, what we now call the "mind" was known to the ancients as the "spirit" or the "soul."[157] This is why the first Christians, the Gnostics, rightly said: "God is all mind and mind is all God"; and it is also why one of the Gnostic Greek names for God was *Nous* ("Mind").[158]

This same unified Mind, your spiritual essence, has many other names, of course, one of the most famous being the great "I AM." The Old Testament, for instance, gives this name to God the Father.[159] What does I AM mean? Precisely what it says. If your "soul" (your mind) is from the Father, and the Christ is in you, and you are in the Christ, and the Christ is in the Father,[160] then truly "you and the Father are one"—just as Jesus passionately asserted.[161] Simply put, the I AM is the real you ("I am me"), for it is a piece of God imbued with the Light of Christ (eternal life).

All of the words and phrases above refer to what has also been called God Realization: the discovery, knowledge (that is, gnosis), and understanding that at the core of each one of us we are nonmaterial beings created in the image of a transcendent, creative, super intelligence that, for lack of a better word, believers call "God" and nonbelievers call "Nature." We are, in fact, little individual shards of immaterial light, each one of us using physical bodies as temporary storage vehicles during our mortal lifetimes here on earth. Thus St. John makes reference to "the true light which lighteth every man that cometh into the world."[162] The "light" John speaks of is what we are made of, for as this same Apostle also states, "God is light,"[163] that is, mind, and we are made from this mental light. Jesus too commented on this psychological luminescence: "While ye have light, believe in the light, that ye may be the children of light."[164] This light is the inner divinity that is possessed by all people, and believing in this truth makes you a "child of light."

The ancients innately understood what it took modern scientists thousands of years to discover: "Mass and energy cannot be destroyed, but only converted from one form to another," a law established by Albert Einstein in 1905 and codified in his famous equation $E = mc^2$.[165] Truly, we are immortal light energy impermanently encased in material form for our brief journey on earth.[166] This is why, after we "kick the frame," as the Hindus describe physical death,[167] we carry on for all eternity in spiritual, that is, mental, form.

While all religions preach the doctrine of Theosis in one form or another, we are here mainly concerned with the Judeo-Christian teaching, and—despite the orthodox Church's vigorous attempt to stamp it out—it is not difficult to find, for our Holy Bible brims with references to this spectacular doctrine.

For instance, quoting the Old Testament,[168] Jesus announced: "Is it not written in your law, 'I said, you are gods?'"[169] Christian mystic St. Paul declared that "Christ is all and in all,"[170] "Christ liveth in me,"[171] and "Christ is in me."[172] Of the countless other scriptures that could be given, perhaps the best known example is from the Book of Genesis:

> "Then God said, 'Let us make man in our image, according to our likeness. They will rule over the fish of the sea, the birds of the sky, the livestock, the whole earth, and the creatures that crawl on the earth.' So *God created mankind in his own image*; he created him in the image of God; he created them male and female"[173]

Understanding ancient holy figures like Jesus as personifications of profound esoteric doctrines is actually the key to understanding *all* sacred Christian scripture, which is why Christian mystics have been reading the Bible in this way for thousands of years. In fact, as a deeply mystical work, very little in our Holy Book should be taken literally. Most of it is comprised of sacred symbols, allegories, signs, numbers, metaphors, tokens, ciphers, myths, devices, emblems, cryptonyms, parables, glyphs, fables, totems, icons, ideograms, logographs, and other occult figurative representations. St. Paul admits as much in his letter to the

Galatians.[174]

Is it not blatantly obvious to all but the least informed that the canonical life story of Jesus, including his connections to the 12 Apostles,[175] as well as that of the Virgin Mary "clothed with the Sun," standing on a crescent moon while wearing a crown of 12 stars,[176] is all allegorical in nature, mystically connected to the winter solstice (the "rebirth" of the sun), astrology, the Sun ("Son"), the 12 astrological star signs, and the constellation Virgo (the "Virgin")?[177]

Why was the Bible, like the Gospel of Thomas, written in a mystical language, one not meant to be interpreted literally, but read intuitively? Jesus, who used a secretive, esoteric, parabolic teaching method Himself, answered the question this way: It is to hide sacred knowledge from the uninitiated, the spiritually unevolved, who might use it for wicked purposes. The following is from the Gospel of Matthew:

> "And the disciples came, and said unto him, 'Why speakest thou unto them in parables?'
> "Jesus answered and said unto them, 'Because it is given unto you to know the mysteries of the kingdom of heaven, but to them it is not given. For whosoever hath, to him shall be given, and he shall have more abundance: but whosoever hath not, from him shall be taken away even that he hath. Therefore speak I to them in parables: because they seeing see not; and hearing they hear not, neither do they understand. And in them is fulfilled the prophecy of Esaias, which saith, by hearing ye shall hear, and shall not understand; and seeing ye shall see, and shall not perceive: For this people's heart is waxed gross, and their ears are dull of hearing, and their eyes they have closed; lest at any time they should see with their eyes and hear with their ears, and should understand with their heart, and should be converted, and I should heal them. But blessed are your eyes [Third Eye], for they see: and your ears [Third Ear], for they hear. For verily I say unto you, that many prophets and righteous men have desired to see those things which ye see, and have not seen them; and to hear those things which ye hear, and have not heard them.'"[178]

Jesus the mystic, like His Gnostic Christian followers then as today, wanted to experience God directly. He did not want or need an intermediary between Himself and the Father. He communicated directly with the Source; he knew He was from the Source, that He was one with the Source. He attempted to communicate this Truth to his followers, along with the all-important doctrines of the Kingdom, Theosis, the Law of Attraction, and immortality, among others. Of such wisdom is the Gospel of Thomas comprised.

With all of this in mind, prepare yourself. You are about to enter a literary spiritual realm in which Jesus turns the orthodox Christian world upside down, overriding it with countless occultic statements steeped in ancient pre-Christian mysticism.

Remember the Buddhist koan, and ready your neural receptors for a journey of new, sometimes shocking, spiritual (that is, psychological) revelations. For the Jesus of the Gospel of Thomas is not interested in merely preaching to you or judging you, and He is certainly not interested in converting you. He actually has but one goal: to break open the cell doors of your self-made mental prison, and free you from confirmation bias so that you can discover the splendors of the Kingdom of Heaven in your own manner and time.

It all began in the land known as the "Light of the World": ancient Egypt.

Once you enter this supernatural domain you will understand, quite possibly for the first time in your life, the real truth behind the "Good News" of the Gospels. Be clear that it is not what you have been taught, for Spiritual Truth cannot be taught, explained, or understood logically. Hence, you will not find it in this book, or in any other book. No educator can teach it to you. No guru can instill it in you. No sage can impart it to you. Spiritual Truth must be found, absorbed, and understood by you and you alone.[179] No intermediaries!

The Gospel of Thomas is a signpost that helps direct seekers who have "ears to hear" and "eyes to see" toward the general vicinity of the front gates of the Kingdom of Heaven. Ultimately finding them and passing through them is up to you.

Ancient star map showing the procession of the constellations with their accompanying deity names. Ancient astrology, along with sun worship, moon worship, and agricultural religions, helped give rise to the Pagan myths that were later appended to the figure of Jesus. See my book, *Christmas Before Christianity*.

NOTES ON THE FOLLOWING CHAPTER

• I do not necessarily claim to agree or disagree with my interpretations of the Gospel of Thomas. I am simply offering one potential rendering of the words of Thomas as I understand them as a Christian mystic.

• Indeed, my interpretations are not the only ones possible. In fact, many dozens if not hundreds of individuals have construed the Gospel of Thomas in their own way and in their own words. The very nature of a mystical, Gnostic-tinged document like Thomas means that there is no one interpretation that is "correct" or "incorrect." Mine, for example, is only intended to help point the uninitiated in a direction where their own interpretation becomes meaningful and beneficial to them.

• Unlike many others, in interpreting Thomas I did not rely on the original languages (e.g., Greek, Coptic, etc.) for assistance in uncovering the meanings of the sayings. Instead, I have simply used the English translation to transmit Thomas' inner esoteric sense, import, and messages. — L.S.

SYMBOLS KEY
• Lacunae and estimations (gaps in the text): [ ]
• Editorial insertions: ( )
• Editorial corrections of scribal errors: / \

According to Jesus Himself, He spoke in parables to protect the sacred knowledge (gnosis) from the spiritually unenlightened.

THE GOSPEL OF THOMAS
ANCIENT TEXT WITH MYSTICAL INTERPRETATIONS

ANCIENT ORIGINAL BY ST. THOMAS
Prologue: These are the secret sayings that the living Jesus spoke and Didymos Judas Thomas wrote down.
MODERN INTERPRETATION BY SEABROOK
Prologue: What follows are the occult teachings of ancient spiritual wisdom, given to the "twins" of Jesus; that is, to all who share in the Mind of Christ possessed by Jesus: Christ Consciousness.

ANCIENT ORIGINAL BY ST. THOMAS
1: And he said, "Whoever discovers the meaning of these sayings won't taste death."
MODERN INTERPRETATION BY SEABROOK
1: Christ Consciousness says that those who uncover the inner meaning of the following statements will realize both their divinity and their immortality.

ANCIENT ORIGINAL BY ST. THOMAS
2: Jesus said, "Whoever seeks shouldn't stop until they find. When they find, they'll be disturbed. When they're disturbed, they'll be […] amazed, and reign over the All."
MODERN INTERPRETATION BY SEABROOK
2: Christ Consciousness says that seekers of the Truth should never give up in their quest until they reach their goal. Yes, what you find may at first seem confusing. But it is that confusion that will eventually free you from your self-imposed bonds, inspiring you, and allowing you entry into the Kingdom of God, where you will have control over all material concerns.

ANCIENT ORIGINAL BY ST. THOMAS
3: Jesus said, "If your leaders tell you, 'Look, the kingdom is in

heaven,' then the birds of heaven will precede you. If they tell you, 'It's in the sea,' then the fish will precede you. Rather, the kingdom is within you and outside of you.

"When you know yourselves, then you'll be known, and you'll realize that you're the children of the living Father. But if you don't know yourselves, then you live in poverty, and you are the poverty."

MODERN INTERPRETATION BY SEABROOK

3: Christ Consciousness says do not listen to what your leaders try to teach you about the Kingdom of Heaven. For it cannot be found where they tell you it is. If they tell you it is in the sky, then the lowly birds will be more spiritually elevated than you; if they tell you it is in the sea, then the lowly fish will be more spiritually advanced than you. How foolish!

Instead, turn inside and get to know your real self; then and only then will you realize your divine nature. If you do not do this, you will live in spiritual poverty, for you are spiritually poor.

ANCIENT ORIGINAL BY ST. THOMAS

4: Jesus said, "The older person won't hesitate to ask a little seven-day-old child about the place of life, and they'll live, because many who are first will be last, and they'll become one."

MODERN INTERPRETATION BY SEABROOK

4: Modern psychologists tell us that we are more deeply impacted by what occurred during infancy and childhood than anything that may occur later on in our lives. Christ Consciousness says the opposite: If a spiritually mature person looks fearlessly back into his or her youthful past, the first half of life will actually be seen as far less impactful than the second half. For, spiritually speaking, what happened in your childhood is not as important as what you are doing, saying, and thinking *right now* as an adult. This is because the Universe/Creative Intelligence/God is always interacting with who you are now, not who you were in the past. Realization of this Truth creates psychological (spiritual) unity—known as individuation or self-realization.

ANCIENT ORIGINAL BY ST. THOMAS
5: Jesus said, "Know what's in front of your face, and what's hidden from you will be revealed to you, because there's nothing hidden that won't be revealed."

MODERN INTERPRETATION BY SEABROOK
5: Christ Consciousness says that intuition, that is, seeing with the inner (third) eye, will always provide an answer to your questions, a solution to your problems. For nothing can hide from spiritual insight.

ANCIENT ORIGINAL BY ST. THOMAS
6: His disciples said to him, "Do you want us to fast? And how should we pray? Should we make donations? And what food should we avoid?"

Jesus said, "Don't lie, and don't do what you hate, because everything is revealed in the sight of heaven; for there's nothing hidden that won't be revealed, and nothing covered up that will stay secret."

MODERN INTERPRETATION BY SEABROOK
6: The unenlightened have been taught that external rituals are the key to getting into Heaven. Christ Consciousness says not to worry about such trivial matters. Rather, focus on avoiding sin and doing what you dislike, for all is visible to Spirit.

ANCIENT ORIGINAL BY ST. THOMAS
7: Jesus said, "Blessed is the lion that's eaten by a human and then becomes human, but how awful for the human who's eaten by a lion, and the lion becomes human."

MODERN INTERPRETATION BY SEABROOK
7: Christ Consciousness says that it is much better for a sinful person to become sinless than for a sinless person to become sinful.

ANCIENT ORIGINAL BY ST. THOMAS
8: He said, "The human being is like a wise fisher who cast a net into the sea and drew it up from the sea full of little fish. Among

them the wise fisher found a fine large fish and cast all the little fish back down into the sea, easily choosing the large fish. Anyone who has ears to hear should hear!"

MODERN INTERPRETATION BY SEABROOK
8: Christ Consciousness says that the wise person focuses on the big spiritual picture, not on small material things. Those who know how to listen to these words with their Third Ear (intuition), let them understand!

ANCIENT ORIGINAL BY ST. THOMAS
9: Jesus said, "Look, a sower went out, took a handful of seeds, and scattered them. Some fell on the roadside; the birds came and gathered them. Others fell on the rock; they didn't take root in the soil and ears of grain didn't rise toward heaven. Yet others fell on thorns; they choked the seeds and worms ate them. Finally, others fell on good soil; it produced fruit up toward heaven, some sixty times as much and some a hundred and twenty."

MODERN INTERPRETATION BY SEABROOK
9: Christ Consciousness says do not waste your time and energy on relationships and jobs that have no hope of a fruitful outcome. This will get you nowhere. Life is short. You and your time are valuable. Be spiritually wise. Invest yourself only in positive, honest, uplifting people and in productive, honest, and uplifting work. Doing this will result in a bountiful spiritual harvest.

ANCIENT ORIGINAL BY ST. THOMAS
10: Jesus said, "I've cast fire on the world, and look, I'm watching over it until it blazes."

MODERN INTERPRETATION BY SEABROOK
10: Christ Consciousness says that individual spiritual enlightenment can only come through the destruction of evil. Be vigilant until this is accomplished.

ANCIENT ORIGINAL BY ST. THOMAS
11: Jesus said, "This heaven will disappear, and the one above it

will disappear too. Those who are dead aren't alive, and those who are living won't die. In the days when you ate what was dead, you made it alive. When you're in the light, what will you do? On the day when you were one, you became divided. But when you become divided, what will you do?"

MODERN INTERPRETATION BY SEABROOK
11: Christ Consciousness says that in order to realize Theosis (one's divine nature) you must completely discard your current thoughts, beliefs, and opinions about life and the world. Throw them out and begin anew. You will never discover your unity with God while thinking in the old way.

ANCIENT ORIGINAL BY ST. THOMAS
12: The disciples said to Jesus, "We know you're going to leave us. Who will lead us then?"

Jesus said to them, "Wherever you are, you'll go to James the Just, for whom heaven and earth came into being."

MODERN INTERPRETATION BY SEABROOK
12: The unenlightened have been taught that there is only one Christ, embodied in the figure of the man known as Jesus of Nazareth.

But Christ Consciousness says that it is not confined to a single person; it is not even limited to human beings specifically. Rather, it is boundless, universal, and omnipresent state of mind, and thus it never "leaves" you. Instead, as St. Paul asserted, any spiritually aware individual can attain the Mind of Christ, which is part of the divine intelligence that created the Universe.

ANCIENT ORIGINAL BY ST. THOMAS
13: Jesus said to his disciples, "If you were to compare me to someone, who would you say I'm like?"

Simon Peter said to him, "You're like a just angel."

Matthew said to him, "You're like a wise philosopher."

Thomas said to him, "Teacher, I'm completely unable to say whom you're like."

Jesus said, "I'm not your teacher. Because you've drunk, you've become intoxicated by the bubbling spring I've measured out."

He took him aside and told him three things. When Thomas returned to his companions, they asked, "What did Jesus say to you?"

Thomas said to them, "If I tell you one of the things he said to me, you'll pick up stones and cast them at me, and fire will come out of the stones and burn you up."

MODERN INTERPRETATION BY SEABROOK

13: The unenlightened have been misled about who Jesus was and what his mission and role were during his short earthly sojourn.

Christ Consciousness says that it cannot be attained or even understood through teaching, reading, studying, discussion, or logical thinking. It can only come through new even radical ways of comprehension and self-introspection, as well as seeing and hearing with the Third Eye and the Third Ear (intuition). There is no one set path for all individuals. Each must come to God Realization in their own time and way—which is why organized religion is so often a serious impediment to spiritual enlightenment, and why metaphysical mystics, like Jesus, do not belong to or espouse a specific religion.

ANCIENT ORIGINAL BY ST. THOMAS

14: Jesus said to them, "If you fast, you'll bring guilt upon yourselves; and if you pray, you'll be condemned; and if you make donations, you'll harm your spirits.

"If they welcome you when you enter any land and go around in the countryside, heal those who are sick among them and eat whatever they give you, because it's not what goes into your mouth that will defile you. What comes out of your mouth is what will defile you.

MODERN INTERPRETATION BY SEABROOK

14: Christ Consciousness says if you wish to attain spiritual enlightenment, do not conform to what conformists tell you to do. Instead, simply do good by being a good person. And remember: What you think, say, and believe are far more important spiritually than what you eat.

ANCIENT ORIGINAL BY ST. THOMAS
15: Jesus said, "When you see the one who wasn't born of a woman, fall down on your face and worship that person. That's your Father."

MODERN INTERPRETATION BY SEABROOK
15: Christ Consciousness says those who have the Mind of Christ understand that their spirit is not "born" and it does not "die." It is immortal, having no birth or death. Only the physical body is born of a man and a woman, and only the physical body dies at the end of its usefulness here on earth. If you meet someone else who knows and accepts this, you two are spiritual siblings, and you should praise and love that person. For God the Father is love.

ANCIENT ORIGINAL BY ST. THOMAS
16: Jesus said, "Maybe people think that I've come to cast peace on the world, and they don't know that I've come to cast divisions on the earth: fire, sword, and war. Where there are five in a house, there'll be three against two and two against three, father against and son and son against father. They'll stand up and be one."

MODERN INTERPRETATION BY SEABROOK
16: Christ Consciousness is the opposite of Church Consciousness or Religious Consciousness. The latter two were invented by human beings and are designed for groups; the former was created by God and is designed for the individual. In short, Christ Consciousness is a purely individualistic state of mind and thus can only be accessed by independent minded, independent thinking individuals. Inevitably then, a person's effort to achieve Christ Consciousness will create division and strife among more mainstream thinking family members, friends, and religions. If they accept and respect one another's differing paths, however, they will remain unified as a family and as friends.

ANCIENT ORIGINAL BY ST. THOMAS
17: Jesus said, "I'll give you what no eye has ever seen, no ear has ever heard, no hand has ever touched, and no human mind has ever thought."

MODERN INTERPRETATION BY SEABROOK
17: Christ Consciousness says that because it is a purely individualistic state of mind, what you will experience when you attain it will be completely different than anyone else who attains it. This is, in great part, why organized religions suppressed the teaching of Christ Consciousness: people with the Mind of Christ, like Jesus, are independent thinkers and thus cannot be controlled.

ANCIENT ORIGINAL BY ST. THOMAS
18: The disciples said to Jesus, "Tell us about our end. How will it come?"

Jesus said, "Have you discovered the beginning so that you can look for the end? Because the end will be where the beginning is. Blessed is the one who will stand up in the beginning. They'll know the end, and won't taste death."

MODERN INTERPRETATION BY SEABROOK
18: The unenlightened have been taught many errors concerning so-called "life" and "death."

Christ Consciousness says that the end of your life, like the beginning of life, will be what you yourself make of it. Those who bravely pursue the wisdom behind this statement will realize their immortality, never fearing the death of the physical body.

ANCIENT ORIGINAL BY ST. THOMAS
19: Jesus said, "Blessed is the one who came into being before coming into being. If you become my disciples and listen to my message, these stones will become your servants; because there are five trees in paradise which don't change in summer or winter, and their leaves don't fall. Whoever knows them won't taste death."

MODERN INTERPRETATION BY SEABROOK
19: Christ Consciousness says that when you attain it, you will know that we are alive before coming to the material world and that will we live on after leaving it. The teachings that come from the Mind of Christ are so powerful that once you learn them you will even have control over inanimate objects. Human beings, with their head and four limbs, are symbolized by the pentagram, or

five-pointed star, itself a changeless emblem of human perfection on earth. Blessed is he or she who realizes their divine perfection, their godhood, and the eternality of the soul.

ANCIENT ORIGINAL BY ST. THOMAS
20: The disciples asked Jesus, "Tell us, what can the kingdom of heaven be compared to?"

He said to them, "It can be compared to a mustard seed. Though it's the smallest of all the seeds, when it falls on tilled soil it makes a plant so large that it shelters the birds of heaven."

MODERN INTERPRETATION BY SEABROOK
20: The unenlightened have been misled concerning the Kingdom of Heaven.

Christ Consciousness explains it this way: The masses regard the Kingdom of Heaven as almost wholly unimportant, and therefore disregard it. This is because it exists only within, and it also because it takes great effort to find it and enter it. Despite this ignorance, the Kingdom is a vitally large and significant gift bestowed upon us by the Father for our edification and pleasure.

ANCIENT ORIGINAL BY ST. THOMAS
21: Mary said to Jesus, "Whom are your disciples like?"

He said, "They're like little children living in a field which isn't theirs. When the owners of the field come, they'll say, 'Give our field back to us.' They'll strip naked in front of them to let them have it and give them their field.

"So I say that if the owner of the house realizes the bandit is coming, they'll watch out beforehand and won't let the bandit break into the house of their domain and steal their possessions. You, then, watch out for the world! Prepare to defend yourself so that the bandits don't attack you, because what you're expecting will come. May there be a wise person among you!

"When the fruit ripened, the reaper came quickly, sickle in hand, and harvested it. Anyone who has ears to hear should hear!"

MODERN INTERPRETATION BY SEABROOK
21: Christ Consciousness says that merely calling yourself a

follower of the Mind of Christ (a Christian) is not enough. If you worship the Christ superficially you are no better than a child playing with a borrowed toy: no one can steal it from him because it is not his to begin with.

Wise is he or she who worships the Christ with their whole being, for their precious beliefs and invaluable knowledge are stored in their own hearts. But they must take care. For there are ignorant people who are jealous of Christ Consciousness and its many gifts, and will try to destroy the bearer and steal his or her spiritual treasures for illicit purposes.

There is no time to lose. If and when you attain Christ Consciousness you must act quickly. Immediately put its teachings into practice in your daily life. All those capable of hearing with their Third Ear, let them listen carefully to the inner meaning of this message.

ANCIENT ORIGINAL BY ST. THOMAS
22: Jesus saw some little children nursing. He said to his disciples, "These nursing children can be compared to those who enter the kingdom."

They said to him, "Then we'll enter the kingdom as little children?"

Jesus said to them, "When you make the two into one, and make the inner like the outer and the outer like the inner, and the upper like the lower, and so make the male and the female a single one so that the male won't be male nor the female female; when you make eyes in the place of an eye, a hand in the place of a hand, a foot in the place of a foot, and an image in the place of an image; then you'll enter [the kingdom]."

MODERN INTERPRETATION BY SEABROOK
22: Christ Consciousness says that you must have the open-mindedness and wide-eyed innocence of a child to enter the Kingdom of Heaven. This is due to the fact that preconceived ideas and beliefs prevent us from experiencing the Mind of Christ. Free thinking, on the other hand, allows access to the inner kingdom by permitting God's spiritual energy to flow effortlessly through our souls. Old beliefs, old habits, and old opinions block this flow.

To help facilitate this process we must disregard our binary material world which is divided into up and down, high and low, ones and twos, inner and outer, right and left, male and female. Focus on the oneness of all things, and the entrance to the Kingdom will manifest itself to you.

ANCIENT ORIGINAL BY ST. THOMAS
23: Jesus said, "I'll choose you, one out of a thousand and two out of ten thousand, and they'll stand as a single one."
MODERN INTERPRETATION BY SEABROOK
23: Christ Consciousness says that very few individuals will achieve it. These people will remain separated from the Divine. But those few who do attain the Mind of Christ will be unified in God.

ANCIENT ORIGINAL BY ST. THOMAS
24: His disciples said, "Show us the place where you are, because we need to look for it."
He said to them, "Anyone who has ears to hear should hear! Light exists within a person of light, and they light up the whole world. If they don't shine, there's darkness."
MODERN INTERPRETATION BY SEABROOK
24: The unenlightened seek spiritual things in the external world. Christ Consciousness says that true Spiritual Light exists only within. Those who possess this inner luminescence shine with the light of God (peace, love, joy) wherever they go. Without this light one lives in spiritual darkness. Let those who know how to listen with their Third Ear hear it!

ANCIENT ORIGINAL BY ST. THOMAS
25: Jesus said, "Love your brother as your own soul. Protect them like the pupil of your eye."
MODERN INTERPRETATION BY SEABROOK
25: Christ Consciousness says that we are all one in Christ. Therefore, we are to look out for one another just as carefully as we safeguard our own eyes.

ANCIENT ORIGINAL BY ST. THOMAS
26: Jesus said, "You see the speck that's in your brother's eye, but you don't see the beam in your own eye. When you get the beam out of your own eye, then you'll be able to see clearly to get the speck out of your brother's eye."

MODERN INTERPRETATION BY SEABROOK
26: Christ Consciousness says to think about our own sins before we criticize others.

ANCIENT ORIGINAL BY ST. THOMAS
27: "If you don't fast from the world, you won't find the kingdom. If you don't make the Sabbath into a Sabbath, you won't see the Father."

MODERN INTERPRETATION BY SEABROOK
27: Christ Consciousness says you must disassociate from the material world in order to find and enter the Kingdom of Heaven, which is purely spiritual. Likewise, you must rest from the material world every seventh day in order to renew and realize your oneness with the divine Creative Intelligence.

ANCIENT ORIGINAL BY ST. THOMAS
28: Jesus said, "I stood in the middle of the world and appeared to them in the flesh. I found them all drunk; I didn't find any of them thirsty. My soul ached for the children of humanity, because they were blind in their hearts and couldn't see. They came into the world empty and plan on leaving the world empty. Meanwhile, they're drunk. When they shake off their wine, then they'll change."

MODERN INTERPRETATION BY SEABROOK
28: Christ Consciousness says that it came to earth to teach humanity, manifesting in Israel in the 1st Century in the human form known as Jesus. But the form found no one eager to be taught. All were spiritually ignorant and therefore blind to the Truth. They were born ignorant and will die ignorant, inebriated with materialism. Only if and when they recover from their hangover will they be able to make the necessary spiritual, mental,

and physical changes necessary to enter the Kingdom of Heaven.

ANCIENT ORIGINAL BY ST. THOMAS
29: Jesus said, "If the flesh came into existence because of spirit, that's amazing. If spirit came into existence because of the body, that's really amazing! But I'm amazed at how [such] great wealth has been placed in this poverty."

MODERN INTERPRETATION BY SEABROOK
29: Christ Consciousness says that if the Father created bodies to house our spirits (minds), that is astounding. If He created our spirits (minds) because he wanted to house us temporarily in physical bodies, that is even more astounding. But either way, the most amazing thing is that He put such valuable spiritual treasure (our minds) into such impoverishment (our physical bodies).

ANCIENT ORIGINAL BY ST. THOMAS
30: Jesus said, "Where there are three deities, they're divine. Where there are two or one, I'm with them."

MODERN INTERPRETATION BY SEABROOK
30: Christ Consciousness says that the idea of the Holy Trinity is divine because it represents the mind ("Father"), body ("Jesus"), and soul ("Holy Spirit"). Where there are gods and goddesses of any number, Christ Consciousness is present.

ANCIENT ORIGINAL BY ST. THOMAS
31: Jesus said, "No prophet is welcome in their own village. No doctor heals those who know them."

MODERN INTERPRETATION BY SEABROOK
31: Christ Consciousness says that if we are too familiar with, for example, a person, idea, or place, we can no longer appreciate their true value or uniqueness. We lose objectivity, and with it, the ability to absorb new information, an all-important step in growing spiritually.

ANCIENT ORIGINAL BY ST. THOMAS
32: Jesus said, "A city built and fortified on a high mountain can't fall, nor can it be hidden."
MODERN INTERPRETATION BY SEABROOK
32: Christ Consciousness says that a life constructed around elevated spiritual values cannot be destroyed. Just as importantly, such a life will shine like a beacon to those around it, serving as an exemplar of what all dedicated Truth seekers can achieve.

ANCIENT ORIGINAL BY ST. THOMAS
33: Jesus said, "What you hear with one ear, listen to with both, then proclaim from your rooftops. No one lights a lamp and puts it under a basket or in a hidden place. Rather, they put it on the stand so that everyone who comes and goes can see its light."
MODERN INTERPRETATION BY SEABROOK
33: Christ Consciousness says that you should freely communicate with others the spiritual lessons you learn by way of intuition and inspiration. For, since it may benefit others, we should never hide our spiritual light (that is, gnosis, "knowledge").

ANCIENT ORIGINAL BY ST. THOMAS
34: Jesus said, "If someone who's blind leads someone else who's blind, both of them fall into a pit."
MODERN INTERPRETATION BY SEABROOK
35: Christ Consciousness says that if the spiritually illiterate follow the spiritually illiterate both will suffer due to their ignorance.

ANCIENT ORIGINAL BY ST. THOMAS
35: Jesus said, "No one can break into the house of the strong and take it by force without tying the hands of the strong. Then they can loot the house."
MODERN INTERPRETATION BY SEABROOK
35: Christ Consciousness says that no one can destroy the fortified soul of one who is pure of heart. The impure, however, are weakened vessels and are therefore easily broken and ruined by

evil.

ANCIENT ORIGINAL BY ST. THOMAS
36: Jesus said, "Don't be anxious from morning to evening or from evening to morning about what you'll wear."

MODERN INTERPRETATION BY SEABROOK
36: Christ Consciousness says that focusing on material minutia is a waste of time and energy. God takes care of these things for you. Instead focus on spiritual things.

ANCIENT ORIGINAL BY ST. THOMAS
37: His disciples said, "When will you appear to us? When will we see you?"

Jesus said, "When you strip naked without being ashamed, and throw your clothes on the ground and stomp on them as little children would, then [you'll] see the Son of the Living One and won't be afraid."

MODERN INTERPRETATION BY SEABROOK
37: The unenlightened believe that the Christ is a physical entity.

Christ Consciousness says, however, that the spiritually immature will never understand the true nonmaterial nature of the Mind of Christ until they strip away and discard all of their preconceived, all too familiar notions. Then and only then will they experience the Truth about the unknowable Creative Intelligence (the "Living One") and Christ Consciousness (the "Son").

ANCIENT ORIGINAL BY ST. THOMAS
38: Jesus said, "Often you've wanted to hear this message that I'm telling you, and you don't have anyone else from whom to hear it. There will be days when you'll look for me, but you won't be able to find me."

MODERN INTERPRETATION BY SEABROOK
38: Christ Consciousness says that this comforting state of mind is very rare on earth, for it is difficult for the materialist to achieve. Unfortunately, with so few possessing it very few are ever exposed

to its reality. Even the minority who hear of it and search for it will never find it. For they look outwardly instead of inwardly.

ANCIENT ORIGINAL BY ST. THOMAS
39: Jesus said, "The Pharisees and the scholars have taken the keys of knowledge and hidden them. They haven't entered, and haven't let others enter who wanted to. So be wise as serpents and innocent as doves."

MODERN INTERPRETATION BY SEABROOK
39: Christ Consciousness says that organized Christianity has stolen and suppressed the keys of gnosis ("knowledge"). In doing so, mainstream Christians have locked themselves out of the Kingdom of Heaven, while simultaneously blocking those who wish to and who are ready to enter. Protect yourself from conventional Christians. In dealing with them be as cautious as a Palestine viper and guileless as an Oriental turtle dove.

ANCIENT ORIGINAL BY ST. THOMAS
40: Jesus said, "A grapevine has been planted outside of the Father. Since it's malnourished, it'll be pulled up by its root and destroyed."

MODERN INTERPRETATION BY SEABROOK
40: Christ Consciousness says those who follow organized religion live by manmade doctrines instead of those instituted by the Divine Creative Intelligence. Thus, they starve themselves spiritually, suffering unnecessarily due to their unknowingness.

ANCIENT ORIGINAL BY ST. THOMAS
41: Jesus said, "Whoever has something in hand will be given more, but whoever doesn't have anything will lose even what little they do have."

MODERN INTERPRETATION BY SEABROOK
41: Christ Consciousness says that one of its major doctrines is the Law of Reciprocity—that is, the eternal law of "like attracts like." Better known today as the Law of Attraction, it teaches that those

who constantly think of abundance, for instance, will attract abundance and positive experiences. Conversely, those who constantly think of deprivation will attract loss and negative experiences. In short, we attract what we think, believe, and say.[180]

ANCIENT ORIGINAL BY ST. THOMAS
42: Jesus said, "Become passersby."
MODERN INTERPRETATION BY SEABROOK
42: Christ Consciousness says do not become attached to the material world. Instead, live your earthly life as a tourist.

ANCIENT ORIGINAL BY ST. THOMAS
43: His disciples said to him, "Who are you to say these things to us?"
"You don't realize who I am from what I say to you, but you've become like those Judeans who either love the tree but hate its fruit, or love the fruit but hate the tree."
MODERN INTERPRETATION BY SEABROOK
43: The unenlightened do not respect the esoteric I AM doctrines that are "taught" by way of the Mind of Christ (that is, by intuition). They are so spiritually immature that they can only comprehend learning from physical human teachers and books written by others.
Christ Consciousness says that such individuals have divided shallow minds. They are the kind of people who, for example, love the way a person looks but hate the person, or love the person and hate the way the person looks.

ANCIENT ORIGINAL BY ST. THOMAS
44: Jesus said, "Whoever blasphemes the Father will be forgiven, and whoever blasphemes the Son will be forgiven, but whoever blasphemes the Holy Spirit will not be forgiven, neither on earth nor in heaven."
MODERN INTERPRETATION BY SEABROOK
44: Christ Consciousness says that the most sacred aspect of the Holy Trinity is not the Divine Creative Intelligence (the "Father")

or the bodily vehicle we live in while on earth (the "Son"). It is the mind (the "Holy Spirit"), the consecrated spiritual light that forms the core of each living creature. Thus whoever insults the former two will be forgiven. But whoever insults the latter will not be forgiven, either during his or her life on earth or after they return to heaven.

ANCIENT ORIGINAL BY ST. THOMAS
45: Jesus said, "Grapes aren't harvested from thorns, nor are figs gathered from thistles, because they don't produce fruit. [A person who's good] brings good things out of their treasure, and a person who's [evil] brings evil things out of their evil treasure. They say evil things because their heart is full of evil."

MODERN INTERPRETATION BY SEABROOK
45: Christ Consciousness says that the Law of Attraction reigns supreme on both earth and in heaven. The way it works is simple: You attract into your life what you think, believe, and say. Thus spiritually mature people produce superior lives and attract positive experiences, while spiritually immature people produce inferior lives and attract negative experiences.

ANCIENT ORIGINAL BY ST. THOMAS
46: Jesus said, "From Adam to John the Baptizer, no one's been born who's so much greater than John the Baptizer that they shouldn't avert their eyes. But I say that whoever among you will become a little child will know the kingdom and become greater than John."

MODERN INTERPRETATION BY SEABROOK
46: Christ Consciousness says that no one who has ever lived has been as moral and upright as John the Baptist. Despite this, those who are able to cast off their confirmation bias will find entrance to the Kingdom of Heaven, and in doing so will become greater than even John the Baptist.

ANCIENT ORIGINAL BY ST. THOMAS
47: Jesus said, "It's not possible for anyone to mount two horses or stretch two bows, and it's not possible for a servant to follow two leaders, because they'll respect one and despise the other.

"No one drinks old wine and immediately wants to drink new wine. And new wine isn't put in old wineskins, because they'd burst. Nor is old wine put in new wineskins, because it'd spoil.

"A new patch of cloth isn't sewn onto an old coat, because it'd tear apart."

MODERN INTERPRETATION BY SEABROOK
47: Christ Consciousness says that one cannot advance spiritually while still laboring under the beliefs, ideas, rituals, practices, and doctrines that were earlier imposed on them by conventional religion. This is because authentic spirituality and organized religion are complete opposites. Just as you would never store fresh clean wine in an old dirty bottle, a mind that is filled with preconceived religious concepts can never advance on the path toward spiritual enlightenment.

ANCIENT ORIGINAL BY ST. THOMAS
48: Jesus said, "If two make peace with each other in a single house, they'll say to the mountain, 'Go away,' and it will."

MODERN INTERPRETATION BY SEABROOK
48: Christ Consciousness says that two spiritually unified individuals will have power over the laws of physics.

ANCIENT ORIGINAL BY ST. THOMAS
49: Jesus said, "Blessed are those who are one – those who are chosen, because you'll find the kingdom. You've come from there and will return there."

MODERN INTERPRETATION BY SEABROOK
49: Christ Consciousness says that those who attain self-actualization or enlightenment (realization of or oneness with the Divine Self) will most assuredly also discover the entrance to the Kingdom of Heaven—the place of their origins and the place of their eventual homecoming.

ANCIENT ORIGINAL BY ST. THOMAS

50: Jesus said, "If they ask you, 'Where do you come from?' tell them, 'We've come from the light, the place where light came into being by itself, [established] itself, and appeared in their image.'

"If they ask you, 'Is it you?' then say, 'We are its children, and we're chosen by our living Father.'

"If they ask you, 'What's the sign of your Father in you?' then say, 'It's movement and rest.'"

MODERN INTERPRETATION BY SEABROOK

50: Christ Consciousness says we all got our start in the Light, the location of all creation itself, and wherein we were imbued with the Light (our minds). The Father is in us, so we are all children of the Light, chosen by the Creative Intelligence ("Father") to temporarily incarnate on earth. Every cell in our bodies, every movement, is actuated by God's spiritual energy.

ANCIENT ORIGINAL BY ST. THOMAS

51: His disciples said to him, "When will the dead have rest, and when will the new world come?"

He said to them, "What you're looking for has already come, but you don't know it."

MODERN INTERPRETATION BY SEABROOK

51: The unenlightened do not understand life and death, nor do they comprehend the idea of the "new world." They believe it to be a physical realm, one that is set in the future.

Christ Consciousness says the new world is not material. It is spiritual, and everyone who attains the Mind of Christ is already living in it. This is why materialists will never understand it.

ANCIENT ORIGINAL BY ST. THOMAS

52: His disciples said to him, "Twenty-four prophets have spoken in Israel, and they all spoke of you."

He said to them, "You've ignored the Living One right in front of you, and you've talked about those who are dead."

MODERN INTERPRETATION BY SEABROOK

52: The spiritually unenlightened place much importance on the ancient prophecies of the long deceased.

Christ Consciousness says that these individuals mistakenly continue to overlook the Living Word, which is omnipresent, ageless, unalterable, and everlasting.

ANCIENT ORIGINAL BY ST. THOMAS
53: His disciples said to him, "Is circumcision useful, or not?"

He said to them, "If it were useful, parents would have children who are born circumcised. But the true circumcision in spirit has become profitable in every way."

MODERN INTERPRETATION BY SEABROOK
53: The unenlightened continue to focus on the materiality of ritual circumcision.

Christ Consciousness, however, says that physical circumcision is meaningless, while spiritual circumcision (a profound change of heart and mind) is the only true rite that will profit a soul.

ANCIENT ORIGINAL BY ST. THOMAS
54: Jesus said, "Blessed are those who are poor, for yours is the kingdom of heaven."

MODERN INTERPRETATION BY SEABROOK
54: Christ Consciousness says that it is easier for the poor of heart (the humble) to enter the state of mind known as the Kingdom of Heaven than it is for the proud. This is because the minds of humble individuals are less encumbered with preconceptions than arrogant people.

ANCIENT ORIGINAL BY ST. THOMAS
55: Jesus said, "Whoever doesn't hate their father and mother can't become my disciple, and whoever doesn't hate their brothers and sisters and take up their cross like I do isn't worthy of me."

MODERN INTERPRETATION BY SEABROOK
55: Christ Consciousness says that if you place your family relations above your search to discover your oneness with the Divine (Theosis) you will never enter the Kingdom of Heaven.

ANCIENT ORIGINAL BY ST. THOMAS
56: Jesus said, "Whoever has known the world has found a corpse. Whoever has found a corpse, of them the world isn't worthy."
MODERN INTERPRETATION BY SEABROOK
56: Christ Consciousness says that souls who choose to incarnate on earth earn a special status in heaven that places them above those who never choose an earthly incarnation.

ANCIENT ORIGINAL BY ST. THOMAS
57: Jesus said, "My Fathers' kingdom can be compared to someone who had [good] seed. Their enemy came by night and sowed weeds among the good seed. The person didn't let anyone pull out the weeds, 'so that you don't pull out the wheat along with the weeds,' they said to them. 'On the day of the harvest, the weeds will be obvious. Then they'll be pulled out and burned.'"
MODERN INTERPRETATION BY SEABROOK
57: Christ Consciousness says that the pursuit to enter the Kingdom of Heaven is filled with unqualified (sinful) individuals trying to sneak past the guards at the front gate. However, these people will be exposed on the Day of Judgement and will pay the price for their dishonesty.

ANCIENT ORIGINAL BY ST. THOMAS
58: Jesus said, "Blessed is the person who's gone to a lot of trouble. They've found life."
MODERN INTERPRETATION BY SEABROOK
58: Christ Consciousness says that entering the Kingdom of Heaven is not easy. In fact, it is very difficult. Thus, those who work hard at it will be rewarded with the secret of life.

ANCIENT ORIGINAL BY ST. THOMAS
59: Jesus said, "Look for the Living One while you're still alive. If you die and then try to look for him, you won't be able to."
MODERN INTERPRETATION BY SEABROOK
59: Christ Consciousness says that one of the main purposes of

physical incarnation is to discover our oneness with God (Theosis) and gain entrance into the Kingdom of Heaven (enlightenment), both while we are still living on the material plane. After we return to heaven (physical death) it will be too late, however, for in the Spirit Realm we automatically enter the Kingdom of Heaven and are automatically unified with the Living One. The test is occurring here and now.

ANCIENT ORIGINAL BY ST. THOMAS
60: They saw a Samaritan carrying a lamb to Judea. He said to his disciples, "What do you think he's going to do with that lamb?"

They said to him, "He's going to kill it and eat it."

He said to them, "While it's living, he won't eat it, but only after he kills it and it becomes a corpse."

They said, "He can't do it any other way."

He said to them, "You, too, look for a resting place, so that you won't become a corpse and be eaten."

MODERN INTERPRETATION BY SEABROOK
60: Christ Consciousness says be like the wise (the spiritually mature): They are meek as a lamb, yet they are careful to avoid falling into the snares of materialism, which weakens the soul and destroys the body, after which they are consumed by predators (the spiritually immature).

ANCIENT ORIGINAL BY ST. THOMAS
61: Jesus said, "Two will rest on a couch. One will die, the other will live."

Salome said, "Who are you, Sir, to climb onto my couch and eat off my table as if you're from someone?"

Jesus said to her, "I am the one who exists in equality. Some of what belongs to my Father was given to me."

"I'm your disciple."

"So I am telling you, if someone is /equal\, they'll be full of light; but if they're divided, they'll be full of darkness."

MODERN INTERPRETATION BY SEABROOK
61: Christ Consciousness says that only those who seek and

discover their equality with the Divine (the I AM) will find true happiness. Those who continue to believe that they are separate (divided) from God will suffer.

ANCIENT ORIGINAL BY ST. THOMAS
62: Jesus said, "I tell my mysteries to [those who are worthy of my] mysteries. Don't let your left hand know what your right hand is doing."

MODERN INTERPRETATION BY SEABROOK
62: Christ Consciousness says that only the spiritually mature will show interest in or understand the sacred mysteries of the Kingdom of Heaven: Theosis, the great I AM, the Christ Within, Self-Christhood, the Living One, the Law of Attraction, the Inner Light, self-realization, and enlightenment. Thus some things must be kept hidden from the masses (the spiritually unevolved).

ANCIENT ORIGINAL BY ST. THOMAS
63: Jesus said, "There was a rich man who had much money. He said, 'I'll use my money to sow, reap, plant, and fill my barns with fruit, so that I won't need anything.' That's what he was thinking to himself, but he died that very night. Anyone who has ears to hear should hear!"

MODERN INTERPRETATION BY SEABROOK
63: Christ Consciousness says that we should not wait for the "right time" to discover our divinity and enter the Kingdom. Begin now. There is no time to lose. Anyone who knows how to listen with his or her Third Ear (intuition), let them hear and understand!

ANCIENT ORIGINAL BY ST. THOMAS
64: Jesus said, "Someone was planning on having guests. When dinner was ready, they sent their servant to call the visitors.

"The servant went to the first and said, 'My master invites you.'

"They said, 'Some merchants owe me money. They're coming tonight. I need to go and give them instructions. Excuse me from the dinner.'

"The servant went to another one and said, 'My master invites you.'

"They said, "I've just bought a house and am needed for the day. I won't have time.'

"The servant went to another one and said, 'My master invites you.'

"They said, 'My friend is getting married and I'm going to make dinner. I can't come. Excuse me from the dinner.'

"The servant went to another one and said, 'My master invites you.'

"They said, "I've just bought a farm and am going to collect the rent. I can't come. Excuse me.'

"The servant went back and told the master, 'The ones you've invited to the dinner have excused themselves.'

"The master said to their servant, 'Go out to the roads and bring whomever you find so that they can have dinner.'

"Buyers and merchants won't [enter] the places of my Father."

MODERN INTERPRETATION BY SEABROOK

64: Christ Consciousness says the rich, the well-fed, and the materially preoccupied will find it extremely difficult to enter the Kingdom of Heaven. They are focused on the *external* world. It will be much easier for the poor, the malnourished, and the simple to discover their oneness with God. They are much closer to the *internal* world.

ANCIENT ORIGINAL BY ST. THOMAS

65: He said, "A [creditor] owned a vineyard. He leased it out to some sharecroppers to work it so he could collect its fruit.

"He sent his servant so that the sharecroppers could give him the fruit of the vineyard. They seized his servant, beat him, and nearly killed him.

"The servant went back and told his master. His master said, 'Maybe he just didn't know them.' He sent another servant, but the tenants beat that one too.

"Then the master sent his son, thinking, 'Maybe they'll show some respect to my son.'

"Because they knew that he was the heir of the vineyard, the sharecroppers seized and killed him. Anyone who has ears to hear should hear!"

MODERN INTERPRETATION BY SEABROOK
65: Christ Consciousness says to take care when associating with, interacting with, or working with the spiritually immature. They do not respect the sacred Life Force.

ANCIENT ORIGINAL BY ST. THOMAS
66: Jesus said, "Show me the stone the builders rejected; that's the cornerstone."

MODERN INTERPRETATION BY SEABROOK
66: Christ Consciousness says that the most important spiritual teachings and revelations will come from individuals whom society deems the least interesting and the least important.

ANCIENT ORIGINAL BY ST. THOMAS
67: Jesus said, "Whoever knows everything, but is personally lacking, lacks everything."

MODERN INTERPRETATION BY SEABROOK
67: Christ Consciousness says that knowledge gained through intellect is far less important than knowledge (*gnosis*) gained through intuition. In other words, book knowledge is inferior to heart knowledge.

ANCIENT ORIGINAL BY ST. THOMAS
68: Jesus said, "Blessed are you when you're hated and persecuted, and no place will be found where you've been persecuted."

MODERN INTERPRETATION BY SEABROOK
68: Christ Consciousness says happy are those who have been humbled through adversity, but who have not become angry, jaded, and bitter.

ANCIENT ORIGINAL BY ST. THOMAS
69: Jesus said, "Blessed are those who've been persecuted in their

own hearts. They've truly known the Father. Blessed are those who are hungry, so that their stomachs may be filled."

MODERN INTERPRETATION BY SEABROOK
69: Christ Consciousness says happy are those who strive to be righteous. They truly understand their oneness with the Divine. Happy are those who hunger for spiritual knowledge. They will be satiated.

ANCIENT ORIGINAL BY ST. THOMAS
70: Jesus said, "If you give birth to what's within you, what you have within you will save you. If you don't have that within [you], what you don't have within you [will] kill you."

MODERN INTERPRETATION BY SEABROOK
70: Christ Consciousness says that if you recognize your divinity it will greatly enhance your life. If you never attain Theosis it will greatly impair your life.

ANCIENT ORIGINAL BY ST. THOMAS
71: Jesus said, "I'll destroy [this] house, and no one will be able to build it [...?]"

MODERN INTERPRETATION BY SEABROOK
71: Christ Consciousness says that the house known as manmade religion is poorly constructed and will ultimately fall before the forces unleashed by spiritual Truth; that is, sacred religionless teachings that derive from the Mind of Christ.

ANCIENT ORIGINAL BY ST. THOMAS
72: [Someone said to him], "Tell my brothers to divide our inheritance with me."

He said to him, "Who made me a divider?"

He turned to his disciples and said to them, "Am I really a divider?"

MODERN INTERPRETATION BY SEABROOK
72: Christ Consciousness says that Theosis is one of God's greatest and most sacred gifts to humanity. It is therefore not to be used in

a mundane manner.

ANCIENT ORIGINAL BY ST. THOMAS
73: Jesus said, "The harvest really is plentiful, but the workers are few. So pray that the Lord will send workers to the harvest."

MODERN INTERPRETATION BY SEABROOK
73: Christ Consciousness says that its many benefits are obvious and are overflowing all over the world. Yet, because the spiritually immature far outnumber the spiritually mature, few are aware of this amazing bounty. Let us pray for more individuals to come into self-realization and help spread the word.

ANCIENT ORIGINAL BY ST. THOMAS
74: He said, "Lord, many are gathered around the well, but there's nothing to drink."

MODERN INTERPRETATION BY SEABROOK
74: Christ Consciousness says that the spiritually dead flock to organized religion, an empty well.

ANCIENT ORIGINAL BY ST. THOMAS
75: Jesus said, "Many are waiting at the door, but those who are one will enter the bridal chamber."

MODERN INTERPRETATION BY SEABROOK
75: Christ Consciousness says that many people seek happiness in life, but they have not yet discovered the great I AM, their self-Christhood, their unity with the Living God. Only those who have found their oneness with the Divine will reap fulfillment in this life as well as the one hereafter.

ANCIENT ORIGINAL BY ST. THOMAS
76: Jesus said, "The Father's kingdom can be compared to a merchant with merchandise who found a pearl. The merchant was wise; they sold their merchandise and bought that single pearl for themselves.

"You, too, look for the treasure that doesn't perish but

endures, where no moths come to eat and no worms destroy."
MODERN INTERPRETATION BY SEABROOK
76: Christ Consciousness asks, what is the Kingdom of Heaven like? And it answers: The Father's Realm is filled with treasure; not material treasure, but spiritual treasure, which is far more valuable and which never deteriorates.

ANCIENT ORIGINAL BY ST. THOMAS
77: Jesus said, "I'm the light that's over all. I am the All. The All has come from me and unfolds toward me.
"Split a log; I'm there. Lift the stone, and you'll find me there."
MODERN INTERPRETATION BY SEABROOK
77: Christ Consciousness says that the Divine Light of the great I AM is everywhere, for it is in all things and is, in fact, all things. This is why if you cut open a log, you will find the Christ; and if you pick up a rock, you will find the Christ. The Christ energy, the sacred pantheistic source of all, is truly ubiquitous and omnipresent.

ANCIENT ORIGINAL BY ST. THOMAS
78: Jesus said, "What did you go out into the desert to see? A reed shaken by the wind? A [person] wearing fancy clothes, [like your] rulers and powerful people? They (wear) fancy [clothes], but can't know the truth."
MODERN INTERPRETATION BY SEABROOK
78: Christ Consciousness says it is useless to physically travel in search of the Mind of Christ. And you will not discover it from the wealthy. Only the inner-directed will ever come to know the Truth.

ANCIENT ORIGINAL BY ST. THOMAS
79: A woman in the crowd said to him, "Blessed is the womb that bore you, and the breasts that nourished you."
He said to [her], "Blessed are those who have listened to the message of the Father and kept it, because there will be days when

you'll say, 'Blessed is the womb that didn't conceive and the breasts that haven't given milk.'"

MODERN INTERPRETATION BY SEABROOK
79: Christ Consciousness says, why callest thou me good? There is none good but one, that is, God. Far happier are those who follow after the Living One, the undefinable Creative Intelligence. His message will greatly aid you during those trying future times when evil forces denounce motherhood while promoting promiscuity and the killing of fetuses.

ANCIENT ORIGINAL BY ST. THOMAS
80: Jesus said, "Whoever has known the world has found the body; but whoever has found the body, of them the world isn't worthy."

MODERN INTERPRETATION BY SEABROOK
80: (Same as Saying 56.) Christ Consciousness says that souls who choose to incarnate on earth earn a special status in heaven that places them above those who never choose an earthly incarnation.

ANCIENT ORIGINAL BY ST. THOMAS
81: Jesus said, "Whoever has become rich should become a ruler, and whoever has power should renounce it."

MODERN INTERPRETATION BY SEABROOK
81: Christ Consciousness says that seeking material success without the spiritual power of the Mind of Christ to support you is useless.

ANCIENT ORIGINAL BY ST. THOMAS
82: Jesus said, "Whoever is near me is near the fire, and whoever is far from me is far from the kingdom."

MODERN INTERPRETATION BY SEABROOK
82: Christ Consciousness says that only those who search for, find, and enter the Kingdom of Heaven will experience the comforting love of the Divine. Those who forsake the Kingdom will be forsaken by God.

ANCIENT ORIGINAL BY ST. THOMAS
83: Jesus said, "Images are revealed to people, but the light within them is hidden in the image of the Father's light. He'll be revealed, but his image will be hidden by his light."

MODERN INTERPRETATION BY SEABROOK
83: Christ Consciousness says that the Father, the supernatural Creative Intelligence, can only be felt, not seen. This is because the Divine is not a person or a physical entity. It is an invisible unfathomable universal energy.

ANCIENT ORIGINAL BY ST. THOMAS
84: Jesus said, "When you see your likeness, you rejoice. But when you see your images that came into being before you did – which don't die, and aren't revealed – how much you'll have to bear!"

MODERN INTERPRETATION BY SEABROOK
84: Christ Consciousness says that everyone is happy when they see their image in a mirror or when they view a photo of themselves. But what about those images of us that were made during our previous life in heaven? These images are eternal, yet we have not seen them from our viewpoint here on earth. How amazed we will be when we finally witness them for the first time!

ANCIENT ORIGINAL BY ST. THOMAS
85: Jesus said, "Adam came into being from a great power and great wealth, but he didn't become worthy of you. If he had been worthy, [he wouldn't have tasted] death."

MODERN INTERPRETATION BY SEABROOK
85: Christ Consciousness says that the first people on earth had the potential to live happy fulfilling lives, and for all eternity—except for one important detail: They ignored the Divine, which made them unfit for immortality.

ANCIENT ORIGINAL BY ST. THOMAS
86: Jesus said, "[The foxes have dens] and the birds have nests, but the Son of Humanity has nowhere to lay his head and rest."

MODERN INTERPRETATION BY SEABROOK
86: Christ Consciousness says that because we humans are spiritual beings not material bodies, the earth is not our true home. Therefore we will never feel completely at home here.

ANCIENT ORIGINAL BY ST. THOMAS
87: Jesus said, "How miserable is the body that depends on a body, and how miserable is the soul that depends on both."

MODERN INTERPRETATION BY SEABROOK
87: Christ Consciousness says that life on the earth plane is not for the weak. It takes great courage and strength to incarnate here.

ANCIENT ORIGINAL BY ST. THOMAS
88: Jesus said, "The angels and the prophets will come to you and give you what belongs to you. You'll give them what you have and ask yourselves, 'When will they come and take what is theirs?'"

MODERN INTERPRETATION BY SEABROOK
88: Christ Consciousness says that the Father will provide the righteous with all that is necessary to live a fulfilling life while here on earth. But at physical death they will be required to leave it all behind.

ANCIENT ORIGINAL BY ST. THOMAS
89: Jesus said, "Why do you wash the outside of the cup? Don't you know that whoever created the inside created the outside too?"

MODERN INTERPRETATION BY SEABROOK
89: Christ Consciousness says that when the mind is pure, the body is pure as well. And when the body is pure, the mind is also pure.

ANCIENT ORIGINAL BY ST. THOMAS
90: Jesus said, "Come to me, because my yoke is easy and my requirements are light. You'll be refreshed."

MODERN INTERPRETATION BY SEABROOK
90: Christ Consciousness says that after acquiring the Mind of

Christ you will find that life's load becomes lighter, for the Christ's demands are few. All who attain it will be renewed.

ANCIENT ORIGINAL BY ST. THOMAS
91: They said to him, "Tell us who you are so that we may trust you."

He said to them, "You read the face of the sky and the earth, but you don't know the one right in front of you, and you don't know how to read the present moment."

MODERN INTERPRETATION BY SEABROOK
91: The unenlightened base their perceptions on the logical mind.

Christ Consciousness says that though the spiritually unaware may be proficient in certain material matters, they have lost the ability to perceive spiritually, that is, intuitively.

ANCIENT ORIGINAL BY ST. THOMAS
92: Jesus said, "Look and you'll find. I didn't answer your questions before. Now I want to give you answers, but you aren't looking for them."

MODERN INTERPRETATION BY SEABROOK
92: Christ Consciousness says that those who sincerely seek after the Kingdom shall find it. But those who do not seek it, will never find it.

ANCIENT ORIGINAL BY ST. THOMAS
93: "Don't give what's holy to the dogs, or else it might be thrown on the manure pile. Don't throw pearls to the pigs, or else they might [...]"

MODERN INTERPRETATION BY SEABROOK
93: Christ Consciousness says do not give anything sacred to the spiritually immature; it will only end up in the trash. And do not share your Christ energy with the spiritually unaware, for they will treat it with contempt, and will probably even try to hurt you.

ANCIENT ORIGINAL BY ST. THOMAS
94: Jesus [said], "Whoever looks will find, [and whoever knocks], it will be opened for them."

MODERN INTERPRETATION BY SEABROOK
94: Christ Consciousness says that all who sincerely search for God's spiritual treasure will find it, and all who knock on the door of wisdom will find it opening wide before them.

ANCIENT ORIGINAL BY ST. THOMAS
95: [Jesus said], "If you have money, don't lend it at interest. Instead, give [it to] someone from whom you won't get it back."

MODERN INTERPRETATION BY SEABROOK
95: Christ Consciousness relies on the Law of Attraction when it comes to money. Example: If you have extra money, do not lend it out. Rather, give it away to someone who you know cannot or will not ever pay you back. According to the Law of Attraction you will eventually receive back ten fold of what you gave away—a much better dividend than lending with interest!

ANCIENT ORIGINAL BY ST. THOMAS
96: Jesus [said], "The Father's kingdom can be compared to a woman who took a little yeast and [hid] it in flour. She made it into large loaves of bread. Anyone who has ears to hear should hear!"

MODERN INTERPRETATION BY SEABROOK
96: Christ Consciousness says that though the Kingdom of Heaven is infinite in all directions, it is its nature to appear tiny and insignificant. Those capable of comprehending by way of the Third Ear (intuition) must pay attention and listen to these words!

ANCIENT ORIGINAL BY ST. THOMAS
97: Jesus said, "The Father's kingdom can be compared to a woman carrying a jar of flour. While she was walking down [a] long road, the jar's handle broke and the flour spilled out behind her on the road. She didn't know it, and didn't realize there was a problem until she got home, put down the jar, and found it empty."

MODERN INTERPRETATION BY SEABROOK
97: Christ Consciousness says that those who live their lives focused on the material will never realize, until its too late, the importance of the Kingdom of Heaven.

ANCIENT ORIGINAL BY ST. THOMAS
98: Jesus said, "The Father's kingdom can be compared to a man who wanted to kill someone powerful. He drew his sword in his house and drove it into the wall to figure out whether his hand was strong enough. Then he killed the powerful one."

MODERN INTERPRETATION BY SEABROOK
98: Christ Consciousness says that one should never underestimate the power of the Kingdom of God.

ANCIENT ORIGINAL BY ST. THOMAS
99: The disciples said to him, "Your brothers and mother are standing outside."

He said to them, "The people here who do the will of my Father are my brothers and mother; they're the ones who will enter my Father's kingdom."

MODERN INTERPRETATION BY SEABROOK
99: The unenlightened believe that biological relationships are real and that they are more important than all else.

Christ Consciousness says, however, that the true family is spiritual not physical, and that it is made up of all those traveling on the Way of Holiness. It is they, our true family members, who will eventually find and enter the Kingdom of Heaven.

ANCIENT ORIGINAL BY ST. THOMAS
100: They showed Jesus a gold coin and said to him, "Those who belong to Caesar demand tribute from us."

He said to them, "Give to Caesar what belongs to Caesar, give to God what belongs to God, and give to me what belongs to me."

MODERN INTERPRETATION BY SEABROOK
100: The unenlightened believe that the most important matter is

paying taxes.

Christ Consciousness says, however, that financial taxes are only one of our vital responsibilities. We must also pay a spiritual tax (that is, live a righteous life) to the Living One, the unknowable Creative Intelligence, as well as one to the Christ, the essence of the entire Universe.

ANCIENT ORIGINAL BY ST. THOMAS
101: "Whoever doesn't hate their [father] and mother as I do can't become my [disciple], and whoever [doesn't] love their [father] and mother as I do can't become my [disciple]. For my mother [...], but [my] true [Mother] gave me Life."

MODERN INTERPRETATION BY SEABROOK
101: (Similar to Saying 55) Christ Consciousness says that those who place more importance on family relationships than on discovering their Inner Divinity will not be able to enter the Kingdom of Heaven. Yes, your earthly mother bore your physical body, but your true Mother, the Female Principle, imbued you with the Life Force.

ANCIENT ORIGINAL BY ST. THOMAS
102: Jesus said, "How awful for the Pharisees who are like a dog sleeping in a feeding trough for cattle, because the dog doesn't eat, and [doesn't let] the cattle eat either."

MODERN INTERPRETATION BY SEABROOK
102: Christ Consciousness says that due to their strict adherence to the manmade tenets and doctrines of Paganized Christianity, orthodox mainstream Christians starve themselves of spiritual sustenance and no longer seek the Kingdom of Heaven. Worse still, they not only prevent other Christians from partaking of the Divine Food, they also block their access to the Kingdom.

ANCIENT ORIGINAL BY ST. THOMAS
103: Jesus said, "Blessed is the one who knows where the bandits are going to enter. [They can] get up to assemble their defenses and

be prepared to defend themselves before they arrive."

MODERN INTERPRETATION BY SEABROOK
103: Christ Consciousness says happy is he or she who knows who the thieves and corruptors of True Religion are. This allows the righteous to guard themselves against their nefarious influences.

ANCIENT ORIGINAL BY ST. THOMAS
104: They said to [Jesus], "Come, let's pray and fast today."
Jesus said, "What have I done wrong? Have I failed?
"Rather, when the groom leaves the bridal chamber, then people should fast and pray."

MODERN INTERPRETATION BY SEABROOK
104: Christ Consciousness says that fasting and praying are most efficacious when the spirit is weak.

ANCIENT ORIGINAL BY ST. THOMAS
105: Jesus said, "Whoever knows their father and mother will be called a bastard."

MODERN INTERPRETATION BY SEABROOK
105: Christ Consciousness says that focusing on earthly biological relationships over heavenly spiritual relationships is a dead end. Such individuals are known to the enlightened as spiritual orphans.

ANCIENT ORIGINAL BY ST. THOMAS
106: Jesus said, "When you make the two into one, you'll become Children of Humanity, and if you say 'Mountain, go away!', it'll go."

MODERN INTERPRETATION BY SEABROOK
106: (Similar to Saying 48) Christ Consciousness says that unifying the conscious mind with the unconscious mind (spiritual individuation) gives one control over the laws of physics, that is, of time and space.

ANCIENT ORIGINAL BY ST. THOMAS
107: Jesus said, "The kingdom can be compared to a shepherd who had a hundred sheep. The largest one strayed. He left the ninety-nine and looked for that one until he found it. Having gone through the trouble, he said to the sheep: 'I love you more than the ninety-nine.'"

MODERN INTERPRETATION BY SEABROOK
107: Christ Consciousness says that authentic spiritual Truth, which derives from the Father, is worth 99 times more than false spiritual truth, which originates in the mind of Man and Woman.

ANCIENT ORIGINAL BY ST. THOMAS
108: Jesus said, "Whoever drinks from my mouth will become like me, and I myself will become like them; then, what's hidden will be revealed to them."

MODERN INTERPRETATION BY SEABROOK
108: Christ Consciousness says that whoever achieves the Mind of Christ will become Christlike, and the sacred mysteries will be made available to them.

ANCIENT ORIGINAL BY ST. THOMAS
109: Jesus said, "The kingdom can be compared to someone who had a treasure [hidden] in their field. [They] didn't know about it. After they died, they left it to their son. The son didn't know it either. He took the field and sold it.

"The buyer plowed the field, [found] the treasure, and began to loan money at interest to whomever they wanted."

MODERN INTERPRETATION BY SEABROOK
109: Christ Consciousness says that those who do not seek and enter the Kingdom of God will lose their promised Divine Inheritance. Those who do seek and find it, however, will prosper.

ANCIENT ORIGINAL BY ST. THOMAS
110: Jesus said, "Whoever has found the world and become rich should renounce the world."

MODERN INTERPRETATION BY SEABROOK
110: Christ Consciousness says that it is especially spiritually dangerous for the wealthy, for they become easily attached to the material world and its seductive trappings. This lifestyle can lead one away from the true source of happiness and eternal life: Spirit.

ANCIENT ORIGINAL BY ST. THOMAS
111: Jesus said, "The heavens and the earth will roll up in front of you, and whoever lives from the Living One won't see death."
Doesn't Jesus say, "Whoever finds themselves, of them the world isn't worthy"?
MODERN INTERPRETATION BY SEABROOK
111: Christ Consciousness says that those who discover the Father Within will realize their immortality. The spiritually unevolved, however, will never understand.

ANCIENT ORIGINAL BY ST. THOMAS
112: Jesus said, "How awful for the flesh that depends on the soul. How awful for the soul that depends on the flesh."
MODERN INTERPRETATION BY SEABROOK
112: (Similar to Saying 87) Christ Consciousness says that incarnating on the earth plane is difficult, and can only be borne by the strong and the courageous.

ANCIENT ORIGINAL BY ST. THOMAS
113: His disciples said to him, "When will the kingdom come?"
"It won't come by looking for it. They won't say, 'Look over here!' or 'Look over there!' Rather, the Father's kingdom is already spread out over the earth, and people don't see it."
MODERN INTERPRETATION BY SEABROOK
113: The spiritually immature believe that God's Kingdom is physical, and that therefore it exists only on earth. Christ Consciousness says, however, that it is not of this world and so it cannot be seen with the physical eyes. Instead, being a spiritual realm, the Kingdom of Heaven exists everywhere and at all times,

imbuing every molecule with the Divine Life Force known as the Living One. Thus it will only be visible to those who see with the Third Eye.

ANCIENT ORIGINAL BY ST. THOMAS

114: Simon Peter said to them, "Mary should leave us, because women aren't worthy of life."

Jesus said, "Look, am I to make her a man? So that she may become a living spirit too, she's equal to you men, because every woman who makes herself manly will enter the kingdom of heaven."

MODERN INTERPRETATION BY SEABROOK

114: The spiritually unevolved believe that the unconscious mind ("woman") is unessential, simultaneously putting all emphasis on the conscious mind ("man").

Christ Consciousness says, however, that the unconscious mind is equal to the conscious mind in value and importance, and that when a person achieves total oneness between the two minds (self-actualization or individuation), he or she will gain access to the Father's Kingdom, a psychological realm where perfect bliss reigns supreme.

The End

Jesus and the Sermon on the Mount.

NOTES

All footnotes, endnotes, & notes in general are mine, unless otherwise indicated. L.S.
(All Bible citations are from the KJV.)

1. Grenfell and Hunt, *New Sayings of Jesus*, p. 22.
2. Hurtado, p. 29.
3. Taylor, p. 81.
4. Coptic is a dialect of the Egyptian language.
5. Robinson, pp. 2, 10, 21-25.
6. Elliot, p. 128.
7. Grant, p. 20.
8. Grenfell and Hunt, *New Sayings of Jesus*, p. 33.
9. Lock and Sanday, p. 16.
10. Evelyn-White, p. xxix.
11. Romans 3:2. See also Acts 7:38; Hebrews 5:12; 1 Peter 4:11, where the word *logion* or "oracle" is also used.
12. Robinson, p. 117.
13. Evelyn-White, p. xxi.
14. Grenfell and Hunt, *New Sayings of Jesus*, p. 25.
15. Evelyn-White. p. lxviii.
16. Robinson, p. 117.
17. Patterson, *The Gospel of Thomas and Jesus*, pp. 113-120.
18. For example, in Matthew 3:2 the KJV has John the Baptist saying: "Repent ye: for the Kingdom of Heaven is at hand." The correct translation is: "Change your minds, for the Kingdom of Heaven is at hand." From Ellis T. Powell, "Spiritualism in Science, Philosophy, and Religion," *Light: A Journal of Spiritual, Psychical and Mystical Research*, No. 2,096, Vol. XLI, March 12, 1921, p. 165.
19. Seabrook, *Jesus and the Law of Attraction*, p. 413.
20. Grenfell and Hunt, *New Sayings of Jesus*, p. 27.
21. See Strong, Greek Dictionary, s.v. "Didumos," 1324, p. 23.
22. See John 20:24-29.
23. See John 20:24. Also see Meyer, p. 97.
24. James, p. 15; DeConick, *Voices of the Mystics*, pp. 74-88.
25. See e.g., Kennett, passim; D'Cruz, passim.
26. See my book, *The Greatest Jesus Mystery of All Time: Where Was Christ Between the Ages of 12 and 30?*
27. Grenfell and Hunt, *New Sayings of Jesus*, p. 33.
28. Lock and Sanday, p. 49.
29. Hurtado, p. 34.
30. Grenfell and Hunt, *New Sayings of Jesus*, pp. 24, 26.
31. Robinson, p. 7. For more on the Essenes and early Christianity, see Fitzmyer, passim.
32. Cowper, p. 128.
33. Grenfell and Hunt, *New Sayings of Jesus*, pp. 22, 29; Montefiore and Turner, p. 21.
34. Zinner, pp. 128-140, 143-150.
35. Montefiore and Turner, p. 11.
36. Hastings, Selbie, and Lambert, Vol. 1, p. 680.
37. Krause, Robinson, and Wisse, p. 6.
38. Lock and Sanday, p. 36.
39. See e.g., A. Walker, pp. ix-x; Andrews, pp. 160-161; Sinker, p. 101; Croce, pp. viii-ix.
40. Burkitt, p. 338.
41. Aune, p. 21.

42. Bennett, p. 627.
43. See e.g., Pick, p. 277. Note: It is assumed by some that the Jesus saying Hippolytus cites in his book is probably the same as Saying 4 in our Gospel of Thomas. If they are one and the same Gospel, this would mean that our Gospel of Thomas was either in circulation during Hippolytus's lifetime or was well-known and often quoted. For a fuller discussion of this problem, see Grenfell and Hunt, *The Oxyrhynchus Papyri*, pp. 18-20; and Hastings, Vol. 1, pp. 485-488.
44. For more on my mystical Christian views, see my book: *Seabrook's Bible Dictionary of Traditional and Mystical Christian Doctrines*.
45. Grant, p. 19.
46. For more on Jesus as a mystic see my book, *Jesus and the Law of Attraction*, passim. For more on the Bible as a mystical work see my books, *Seabrook's Bible Dictionary of Traditional and Mystical Christian Doctrines*, passim, and *The Bible and the Law of Attraction*, passim.
47. See e.g., Evans, *The World of Jesus and the Early Church*, p. 181.
48. Massey, *Ancient Egypt, the Light of the World*, Vol. 2, p. 894.
49. Hastings, Selbie, and Lambert, Vol. 1, p. 680.
50. Grant, p. 20.
51. See DeConick, *The Original Gospel of Thomas in Translation*, p. 2.
52. Cowper, pp. 128-129.
53. Shedd, 107.
54. See e.g., Evelyn-White, pp. xxix-xxx; Robinson, p. 117; Lindemann, p. 155 and passim.
55. See my book: *Jesus and the Gospel of Q: Christ's Pre-Christian Teachings as Recorded in the New Testament*.
56. 2 Corinthians 5:7.
57. Romans 11:33-36.
58. For more on the possible connections between Gnosticism and the Gospel of Thomas, see Ehrman and Pleše, passim.
59. Robinson, p. 17.
60. B. G. Walker, s.v. "Ankh" (pp. 82-83).
61. Robinson, p. 17.
62. B. G. Walker, s.v. "Fish" (p. 374).
63. Robinson, p. 21.
64. Seabrook, *Seabrook's Bible Dictionary of Traditional and Mystical Christian Doctrines*, s.v. "Yahweh"; s.v. "Jehovah."
65. For more on this topic see my book: *Christmas Before Christianity: How the Birthday of the "Sun" Became the Birthday of the "Son."*
66. Priestley, p. vii.
67. Robinson, p. 5.
68. Robinson, p. 5.
69. See Logan, passim.
70. See in particular 1 Galatians and 2 Galatians, as well as the book of Romans.
71. See e.g., Acts 8:9-24; 1 Timothy 6:20; 2 Timothy 2:17.
72. See Grant, p. 20.
73. For associations between Gnosticism and the Nag Hammadi Library as a whole, see Hedrick and Hodgson, passim.
74. Seabrook, *Seabrook's Bible Dictionary of Traditional and Mystical Christian Doctrines*, s.v. "Christ."
75. Grenfell and Hunt, *New Sayings of Jesus*, p. 23.
76. Note that like the Gospel of Thomas and the early layers of the Gospel of Q, the Book of James makes no mention of the supernatural, clearly Paganized, events in Jesus' life—later recorded so sensationally in the four canonical Gospels. Revealingly, in James Jesus is only mentioned twice by name and is portrayed as a very mortal but special human role model.
77. Evelyn-White, pp. xxxv-xxxvii.
78. See Lindemann, p. 155. Some, however, see possible connections between Thomas and the Synoptics. See e.g., Evans, *Jesus and the Manuscripts*, passim.
79. Evelyn-White, pp. xxxiv-xxxv.

80. In astrology the four quarter signs, two equinoxes and two solstices, mark the beginning of each of the four seasons. In Paganism they were (and still are) personified by four compass gods, as follows: Aquarius the water-bearer, who in Christianity became associated with Matthew; Leo the lion, who in Christianity became associated with Mark; Taurus the bull, who in Christianity became associated with Luke; and Aquila the eagle (later, Scorpio the scorpion), who in Christianity became associated with John. For more on the topic of the Christian Tetramorph, see *Seabrook's Bible Dictionary of Traditional and Mystical Christian Doctrines*, s.v. "Tetramorph (Christian)."
81. Patterson, *The Gospel of Thomas and Christian Origins*, p. 96.
82. Evelyn-White, pp. xxix-xxx.
83. Lock and Sanday, p. 31.
84. Valantasis, p. 2.
85. See Acts 20:35.
86. Evelyn-White, p. xxx.
87. Evelyn-White, p. xxxiii.
88. John 21:25.
89. Grenfell and Hunt, *New Sayings of Jesus*, p. 32.
90. Taylor, p. 5.
91. Evelyn-White, p. xxxix.
92. Evelyn-White, p. 3.
93. Grenfell and Hunt, *New Sayings of Jesus*, p. 24.
94. Taylor, p. 82.
95. Evelyn-White, pp. xxxix; xli-xlii.
96. Grenfell and Hunt, *New Sayings of Jesus*, p. 27.
97. Gathercole, pp. 35-53; Elliot, pp. 128-129; Cowper, p. 128; Montefiore and Turner, pp. 14-16.
98. Elliott, p. 24.
99. Evelyn-White, pp. xxvii-xxix.
100. See Luke 1:1-2; John 20:30-31.
101. See e.g., Mark 2:1-3-6; 9:33-50.
102. Luke provides a similar list. See Luke 6:20-49.
103. While it may go without saying as far as New Testament scholars are concerned, it is worth repeating the fact that Jesus died many decades before the earliest known Gospel, Mark, was written.
104. Grant, pp. 24-25.
105. For evidence of Jesus' pre-Gospel sayings collections in Paul, see e.g., 1 Corinthians 7:10-12, 25; 9:14; 11:23-25; 15:3-7.
106. See Matthew 13:1-23; Mark 4:1-20; Luke 8:4-15.
107. Meyer, pp. xix-xx.
108. See John 14:28, where Jesus not only distinctly separates Himself from God, but says of God He is "greater than I."
109. For more on the topic of Jesus' "lost years," see my book, *The Greatest Jesus Mystery of All Time: Where Was Christ Between the Ages of 12 and 30?*
110. See e.g., Matthew 11:28-30, and Gospel of Thomas, Saying 90.
111. Priestley, p. 2.
112. Matthew 13:55.
113. Luke 2:41.
114. Luke 2:48.
115. Luke 3:23.
116. Luke 4:22.
117. John 1:45.
118. John 6:42.
119. Hebrews 3:3.
120. Hebrews 7:24.
121. Hebrews 10:12.
122. Acts 2:22.
123. 1 Timothy 2:5.

124. Priestley, p. 1.
125. John 14:20.
126. John 8:50.
127. Matthew 19:16-17.
128. Priestley, p. 7.
129. Priestley, pp. 3-4, 7; Zinner, p. 182.
130. John 14:12.
131. Priestley, pp. 8-16.
132. Seabrook, *Seabrook's Bible Dictionary of Traditional and Mystical Christian Doctrines*, s.v. "Logos."
133. See John 1:1.
134. For more on this subject see my book, *Christmas Before Christianity: How the Birthday of the "Sun" Became the Birthday of the "Son."*
135. Malachi 4:2.
136. Jefferson, pp. 283-284.
137. Seabrook, *Jesus and the Law of Attraction*, p. 412.
138. Massey, *The Logia of the Lord*, pp. 1-2.
139. For more on this topic see my book, *Jesus and the Law of Attraction*, passim.
140. For more on the topic of the nature of Jesus see my book, *Seabrook's Bible Dictionary of Traditional and Mystical Doctrines*, s.v. "Jesus."
141. Priestley, p. 7.
142. Grenfell and Hunt, *New Sayings of Jesus*, p. 22.
143. Schweitzer, p. 309. See also Bauer, passim.
144. See John 10:36, where there is continuing debate over the line "I am *the* son of God," which should read: "I am *a* son of God."
145. For more on this topic see my book, *Jesus and the Gospel of Q: Christ's Pre-Christian Teachings as Recorded in the New Testament*. Also see Harnack, *The Sayings of Jesus*. passim.
146. E.g., Matthew 9:6; 11:19.
147. Seabrook, *Seabrook's Bible Dictionary of Traditional and Mystical Doctrines*, s.v. "Son of Man."
148. For more on this topic see my book, *Seabrook's Bible Dictionary of Traditional and Mystical Christian Doctrines*.
149. See e.g., Acts 4:26; Revelation 11:15; 12:10.
150. For more on this topic see my book, *Christ is All and in All: Rediscovering Your Divine Nature and the Kingdom Within*.
151. 1 Corinthians 2:16.
152. Romans 8:14.
153. Luke 8:10; John 3:5; Mark 10:15.
154. Matthew 5:3; 7:21; 10:7.
155. See Bucke, passim.
156. Seabrook, *Seabrook's Bible Dictionary of Traditional and Mystical Doctrines*, s.v. "John the Baptist."
157. In Christian mysticism it is believed we possess three bodies: The mind (our true self), is housed in a soul (the usually indistinct whitish entity that is seen as "ghosts" by observers), which is in turn housed in a physical body. Hence, the physical body protects and carries the soul, while the soul protects and carries the mind. For more on this topic see my book, *Seabrook's Bible Dictionary of Traditional and Mystical Doctrines*, s.v. "Soul," s.v. "Spirit," s.v. "Christ," s.v. "Crown," s.v. "Divine Mind," s.v. "God."
158. *Seabrook's Bible Dictionary of Traditional and Mystical Doctrines*, s.v. "Divine Mind."
159. Exodus 3:14.
160. John 14:20.
161. John 10:30. See also 1 John 4:16.
162. John 1:9.
163. 1 John 1:5.
164. John 12:36.
165. U.S. Army Ordnance Center and School, p. 12.
166. For more on this topic see my book, *Your Soul Lives Forever: Documented Case Studies Proving Consciousness Survives Death*.
167. See e.g., Yogananda, Chapter 27.

168. Psalm 82:6.
169. John 10:34.
170. Colossians 3:1-11.
171. Galatians 2:20.
172. 2 Corinthians 11:10.
173. Genesis 1:26-27.
174. Galatians 4:21-24.
175. Matthew 10:2-4.
176. Revelation 12:1-2.
177. For more on this subject see my book, *Christmas Before Christianity: How the Birthday of the "Sun" Became the Birthday of the "Son."* See also Weigall, passim.
178. Matthew 13:10-17.
179. See Matthew 7:13-14.
180. For more on this topic see my books, *Jesus and the Law of Attraction* and *The Bible and the Law of Attraction*.

Jesus said: "The kingdom of heaven is like unto treasure hid in a field; the which when a man hath found, he hideth, and for joy thereof goeth and selleth all that he hath, and buyeth that field" (Matthew 13:44).

BIBLIOGRAPHY

And Suggested Reading

Andrews, Herbert T. *The Apocryphal Books of the Old and New Testament.* London, UK: T. C. and E. C. Jack, 1908.
Audlin, James David. *The Gospel of John: The Original Version in Greek and English.* Chiriqui, Panama: Volcán Barú, 2013.
Aune, David Edward. *The Westminster Dictionary of New Testament and Early Christian Literature and Rhetoric.* Louiseville, KY: Westminster John Knox Press, 2003.
Baikie, James. *Egyptian Papyri and Papyrus-Hunting.* London, UK: Religious Tract Society, 1925.
Bauer, Bruno. *Christ and the Caesars: The Origin of Christianity From the Mythology of Rome and Greece.* Bloomington, IN: Xlibris, 2015.
Bennett, D. M. *The Gods and Religions of Ancient and Modern Times.* 2 vols. New York: self-published, 1881.
Bernard, Andrew. *Other Early Christian Gospels: A Critical Edition of the Surviving Greek Manuscripts.* London, UK: T. and T. Clark, 2007.
Bible Picture Book: New Testament. London, UK: Society for Promoting Christian Knowledge, 1884.
Blackman, Aylward Manley. *The Rock Tombs of Meir.* London, UK: Egypt Exploration Fund, 1915.
Bucke, Richard Maurice. *Cosmic Consciousness: A Study in the Evolution of the Human Mind.* New York: E. P. Dutton and Co., 1901.
Burkitt, Francis Crawford. *The Gospel History and Its Transmission.* 1906. London, UK: T. and T. Clark, 1925 ed.
Burton, Ernest Dewitt, and Shailer Matthews. *The Life of Christ: An Aid to Historical Study and a Condensed Commentary on the Gospels.* Chicago, IL: University of Chicago Press, 1904.
Cowper, Benjamin Harris. *The Apocryphal Gospels and Other Documents Relating to the History of Christ.* London, UK: David Nutt, 1897.
Croce, Angelo Della. *Canonical Histories and Apocryphal Legends Relating to the New Testament.* Milan, Italy: self-published, 1873.
Crossan, John Dominic. *The Historical Jesus: The Life of a Mediterranean Jewish Peasant.* New York: HarperCollins, 1992.
Cumming, John. *The Life and Lessons of Our Lord Unfolded and Illustrated.* London, UK: John F. Shaw and Co., 1864.

Davies, Stevan. *The Gospel of Thomas and Christian Wisdom.* Portland, OR: Bardic Press, 2005.

D'Cruz, F. A. *St. Thomas, the Apostle, in India.* Madras, India: slef-published, 1929.

DeConick, April D. *Voices of the Mystics: Early Christian Discourse in the Gospels of John and Thomas and Other Ancient Christian Literature.* London, UK: T. and T. Clark, 2001.

———. *The Original Gospel of Thomas in Translation: With a Commentary and New English Translation of the Complete Gospel.* London, UK: T. and T. Clark International, 2006.

Doreese, Jean. *The Secret Books of the Egyptian Gnostics: An Introduction to the Recently Discovered Ancient Manuscripts That Rival the Dead Sea Scrolls in Importance.* New York: MJF Books, 1997.

———. *The Discovery of the Nag Hammadi Texts: A Firsthand Account of the Expedition That Shook the Foundations of Christianity.* Rochester, VT: Inner Traditions, 2005.

Dowling, Levi H. *The Aquarian Gospel of Jesus the Christ.* 1907. Santa Monica, CA: DeVorss and Co., 1972 ed.

Ehrman, Bart D., and Zlatko Pleše. *The Other Gospels: Accounts of Jesus From Outside the New Testament.* Oxford, UK: Oxford University Press, 2014.

Elliot, J. K. *The Apocryphal New Testament: A Collection of Apocryphal Christian Literature in an English Translation.* Oxford, UK: Clarendon Press, 1993.

Erman, Adolf. *Life in Ancient Egypt.* London, UK: Macmillan and Co., 1894.

Evans, Craig A. (ed.). *The World of Jesus and the Early Church: Identity and Interpretation in Early Communities of Faith.* Peabody, MA: Hendrickson Publishers, 2011.

———. *Jesus and the Manuscripts: What We Can Learn from the Oldest Texts.* Peabody, MA: Hendrickson Publishers, 2020.

Evelyn-White, Hugh G. (ed.). *The Sayings of Jesus from Oxyrhynchus.* Cambridge, UK: Cambridge University Press, 1920.

Fitzmyer, Joseph A. *The Oxyrhynchus Logoi of Jesus and the Coptic Gospel According to Thomas.* Baltimore, MD: Johns Hopkins University Press, 1959.

———. *The Dead Sea Scrolls and Christian Origins.* Grand Rapids, MI: William B. Eerdmans Publishing Co., 2000.

Foster, Paul (ed.). *The Non-Canonical Gospels.* London, UK: T. and T. Clark, 2007.

Gathercole, Simon. *The Gospel of Thomas: Introduction and Commentary.* Leiden, The Netherlands: Brill, 2014.

Goodacre, Mark. *Thomas and the Gospels: The Case for Thomas's Familiarity with the Synoptics.* Grand Rapids, MI: William B. Eerdmans Publishing Co., 2012.

Grant, Robert, and David Noel Freedman. *The Secret Sayings of Jesus: A*

Modern Translation of the Gospel of Thomas With Commentary. New York: Barnes and Noble Books, 1960.

Graves, Kersey. *The World's Sixteen Crucified Saviors; or Christianity Before Christ.* Boston, MA: Colby and Rich, 1876.

Grenfell, Bernard Pyne, and Arthur Surridge Hunt. *Sayings of Our Lord.* London, UK: Henry Frowde, 1897.

——. *New Sayings of Jesus and Fragment of a Lost Gospel from Oxyrhynchus.* London, UK: Henry Frowde, 1904.

——. *The Oxyrhynchus Papyri.* London, UK: Henry Frowde, 1904.

Guignebert, Charles. *The Christ.* New York: Citadel Press, 1968.

Harley, Timothy. *Moon Lore.* London, UK: Swan Sonnenschein, 1885.

Harnack, Adolf von. *Outlines of the History of Dogma.* 7 vols. London, UK: Hodder and Stoughton, 1892.

——. *What is Christianity?* New York: G. P. Putnam's Sons, 1908.

——. *The Sayings of Jesus: The Second Source of St. Matthew and St. Luke.* New York: G. P. Putnam's Sons, 1908.

——. *Luke the Physician: The Author of the Third Gospel and the Book of Acts.* New York: G. P. Putnam's Sons, 1908.

——. *The Constitution and Law of the Church in the First Two Centuries.* New York: G. P. Putnam's Sons, 1910.

——. *The Origin of the New Testament and the Most Important Consequences of the New Creation.* New York: Macmillan Co., 1925.

Hastings, James. *Dictionary of the Apostolic Church.* 2 vols. New York: Charles Scribner's Sons, 1916.

Hastings, James, John A. Selbie, and John C.. Lambert (eds.). *A Dictionary of Christ and the Gospels.* 2 vols. New York: Charles Scribner's Sons, 1906.

Hedrick, Charles W., and Robert Hodgson, Jr. (eds.). *Nag Hammadi, Gnosticism, and Early Christianity.* Eugene, OR: Wipf and Stock, 1986.

Hulme, Frederick Edward. *The History, Principles and Practice of Symbolism in Christian Art.* London, UK: Swan Sonnenschein and Co., 1891.

Hurtado, Larry W. *The Earliest Christian Artifacts: Manuscripts and Christian Origins.* Grand Rapids, MI: William B. Eerdmans Publishing Co., 2006.

Jackson, John G. *Christianity Before Christ.* Eastford, CT: Martino, 2015.

James, Montague Rhodes. *The Apocryphal New Testament: Being the Apocryphal Gospels, Acts, Epistles, and Apocalypses.* Oxford, UK: Clarendon Press, 1924.

Jameson, Anna. *The History of Our Lord as Exemplified in Works of Art.* London, UK: Longman, Green, Longman, Roberts, and Green, 1865.

Jefferson, Thomas. *The Writings of Thomas Jefferson.* Philadelphia, PA: J. B. Lippincott and Co., 1869.

Kennett, Egbert. *St. Thomas, the Apostle of India: An Enquiry Into the Evidence for His Mission to This Country.* Madras, India: self-published, 1882.

Krause, Martin, James M. Robinson, and Frederik Wisse (eds.). *Nag Hamaddi Studies*. Leiden, The Netherlands: Brill, 1989.

Layton, Bentley. *The Gnostic Scriptures: Ancient Wisdom for the New Age*. New York: Doubleday, 1995.

Lindemann, Andreas (ed.). *The Sayings Source Q and the Historical Jesus*. Leuven, Belgium: Leuven University Press, 2001.

Lock, Walter, and William Sanday. *Two Lectures on the 'Sayings of Jesus' Recently Discovered at Oxyrhynchus*. Delivered at Oxford University, Oxford, UK, October 23, 1897. Oxford, UK: Clarendon Press, 1897.

Logan, Alastair H. B. *The Gnostics: Identifying an Early Christian Cult*. London, UK: T. and T. Clark, 2006.

Massey, Gerald. *The Natural Genesis*. London, UK: Williams and Norgate, 1883.

———. *The 'Logia of the Lord'; or, Pre-historic Sayings Ascribed to Jesus the Christ*. London, UK: self-published, 1887.

———. *Ancient Egypt, the Light of the World: A Work of Reclamation and Restitution in Twelve Books*. London, UK: T. Fisher Unwin, 1907.

McClintock, John, and James Strong. *Cyclopaedia of Biblical, Theological, and Ecclesiastical Literature*. New York: Harper, 1867.

Meagher, James L. *The Great Cathedrals and Most Celebrated Churches of the World*. New York: Peter P. Mulligan, 1923.

Metropolitan Museum of Art. *Art of Ancient Egypt: A Resource for Educators*. New York: 1998.

Meyer, Marvin W. *The Secret Teachings of Jesus: Four Gnostic Gospels*. New York: Vintage, 1984.

———. *Secret Gospels: Essays on Thomas and the Secret Gospel of Mark*. Harrisburg, PA: Trinity Press International, 2003.

Miller, Robert J. (ed.). *The Complete Gospels*. 1992. Oregon, CA: Polebridge Press, 2010 ed.

Milligan, George. *Here and There Among the Papyri*. London, UK: Hodder and Stoughton, 1922.

Montefiore, Hugh, and H. E. W. Turner. *Thomas and the Evangelists*. Eugene, OR: Wipf and Stock, 1962.

Patterson, Stephen J. *The Gospel of Thomas and Jesus*. Oregon, CA: Polebridge Press, 1993.

———. *The Gospel of Thomas and Christian Origins: Essays on the Fifth Gospel*. Leiden, The Netherlands: Brill, 2013.

Pick, Bernhard. *The Extracanonical Life of Christ: Being a Record of the Acts and Sayings of Jesus of Nazareth Drawn From Uninspired Sources*. New York: Funk and Wagnalls, 1903.

———. *Paralipomena: Remains of Gospels and Sayings of Christ*. Chicago, IL: Open Court Publishing Co., 1908.

Porter, Stanley E. *How We Got the New Testament: Text, Transmission,*

Translation. Ada, MI: Baker Academic, 2013.
Priestley, Joseph. *A History of the Corruptions of Christianity.* London, UK: The British and Foreign Unitarian Association, 1871.
Robinson, James M. (ed.). *The Nag Hammadi Library in English.* Leiden, The Netherlands: Brill, 1977.
Schaff, Philip. *A Popular Commentary on the New Testament.* Edinburgh, Scotland: T. and T. Clark, 1880.
Schweitzer, Albert. *The Quest of the Historical Jesus.* 1906. New York: Collier Books, 1968 ed.
Seabrook, Lochlainn. *Aphrodite's Trade: The Hidden History of Prostitution Unveiled.* 1994. Franklin, TN: Sea Raven Press, 2011 ed.
——. *The Goddess Dictionary of Words and Phrases: Introducing a New Core Vocabulary for the Women's Spirituality Movement.* 1997. Franklin, TN: Sea Raven Press, 2010 ed.
——. *Britannia Rules: Goddess-Worship in Ancient Anglo-Celtic Society - An Academic Look at the United Kingdom's Matricentric Spiritual Past.* 1999. Franklin, TN: Sea Raven Press, 2010 ed.
——. *The Book of Kelle: An Introduction to Goddess-Worship and the Great Celtic Mother-Goddess Kelle, Original Blessed Lady of Ireland.* 1999. Franklin, TN: Sea Raven Press, 2010 ed.
——. *Carnton Plantation Ghost Stories: True Tales of the Unexplained from Tennessee's Most Haunted Civil War House!* 2005. Franklin, TN, 2016 ed.
——. *Nathan Bedford Forrest: Southern Hero, American Patriot.* 2007. Franklin, TN, 2010 ed.
——. *Abraham Lincoln: The Southern View.* 2007. Franklin, TN: Sea Raven Press, 2013 ed.
——. *The McGavocks of Carnton Plantation: A Southern History - Celebrating One of Dixie's Most Noble Confederate Families and Their Tennessee Home.* 2008. Franklin, TN, 2011 ed.
——. *Christmas Before Christianity: How the Birthday of the "Sun" Became the Birthday of the "Son."* Franklin, TN: Sea Raven Press, 2010.
——. *A Rebel Born: A Defense of Nathan Bedford Forrest.* 2010. Franklin, TN: Sea Raven Press, 2011 ed.
——. *Everything You Were Taught About the Civil War is Wrong, Ask a Southerner!* 2010. Franklin, TN: Sea Raven Press, 2024 ed.
——. *The Quotable Jefferson Davis: Selections From the Writings and Speeches of the Confederacy's First President.* Franklin, TN: Sea Raven Press, 2011.
——. *The Quotable Robert E. Lee: Selections From the Writings and Speeches of the South's Most Beloved Civil War General.* Franklin, TN: Sea Raven Press, 2011 Sesquicentennial Civil War Edition.
——. *Lincolnology: The Real Abraham Lincoln Revealed In His Own Words.* Franklin, TN: Sea Raven Press, 2011.
——. *The Unquotable Abraham Lincoln: The President's Quotes They Don't Want*

You To Know! Franklin, TN: Sea Raven Press, 2011.

———. *Honest Jeff and Dishonest Abe: A Southern Children's Guide to the Civil War.* Franklin, TN: Sea Raven Press, 2012.

———. *Encyclopedia of the Battle of Franklin - A Comprehensive Guide to the Conflict that Changed the Civil War.* Franklin, TN: Sea Raven Press, 2012.

———. *The Quotable Nathan Bedford Forrest: Selections From the Writings and Speeches of the Confederacy's Most Brilliant Cavalryman.* Spring Hill, TN: Sea Raven Press, 2012.

———. *Forrest! 99 Reasons to Love Nathan Bedford Forrest.* Spring Hill, TN: Sea Raven Press, 2012.

———. *Give 'Em Hell Boys! The Complete Military Correspondence of Nathan Bedford Forrest.* Spring Hill, TN: Sea Raven Press, 2012.

———. *The Constitution of the Confederate States of America Explained: A Clause-by-Clause Study of the South's Magna Carta.* Spring Hill, TN: Sea Raven Press, 2012 Sesquicentennial Civil War Edition.

———. *The Great Impersonator: 99 Reasons to Dislike Abraham Lincoln.* Spring Hill, TN: Sea Raven Press, 2012.

———. *The Old Rebel: Robert E. Lee As He Was Seen By His Contemporaries.* Spring Hill, TN: Sea Raven Press, 2012 Sesquicentennial Civil War Edition.

———. *The Quotable Stonewall Jackson: Selections From the Writings and Speeches of the South's Most Famous General.* Spring Hill, TN: Sea Raven Press, 2012 Sesquicentennial Civil War Edition.

———. *Saddle, Sword, and Gun: A Biography of Nathan Bedford Forrest for Teens.* Spring Hill, TN: Sea Raven Press, 2013.

———. *Jesus and the Law of Attraction: The Bible-Based Guide to Creating Perfect Health, Wealth, and Happiness Following Christ's Simple Formula.* Franklin, TN: Sea Raven Press, 2013.

———. *The Bible and the Law of Attraction: 99 Teachings of Jesus, the Apostles, and the Prophets.* Franklin, TN: Sea Raven Press, 2013.

———. *The Alexander H. Stephens Reader: Excerpts From the Works of a Confederate Founding Father.* Spring Hill, TN: Sea Raven Press, 2013.

———. *The Quotable Alexander H. Stephens: Selections From the Writings and Speeches of the Confederacy's First Vice President.* Spring Hill, TN: Sea Raven Press, 2013 Sesquicentennial Civil War Edition.

———. *Christ Is All and In All: Rediscovering Your Divine Nature and the Kingdom Within.* Franklin, TN: Sea Raven Press, 2014.

———. *Jesus and the Gospel of Q: Christ's Pre-Christian Teachings as Recorded in the New Testament.* Franklin, TN: Sea Raven Press, 2014.

———. *Give This Book to a Yankee! A Southern Guide to the Civil War for Northerners.* Spring Hill, TN: Sea Raven Press, 2014.

———. *The Articles of Confederation Explained: A Clause-by-Clause Study of America's First Constitution.* Spring Hill, TN: Sea Raven Press, 2014.

———. *Confederate Blood and Treasure: An Interview With Lochlainn Seabrook.*

Spring Hill, TN: Sea Raven Press, 2015.

———. *Nathan Bedford Forrest and the Battle of Fort Pillow: Yankee Myth, Confederate Fact*. Spring Hill, TN: Sea Raven Press, 2015.

———. *Everything You Were Taught About American Slavery War is Wrong, Ask a Southerner!* Spring Hill, TN: Sea Raven Press, 2015.

———. *Confederacy 101: Amazing Facts You Never Knew About America's Oldest Political Tradition*. Spring Hill, TN: Sea Raven Press, 2015.

———. *The Great Yankee Coverup: What the North Doesn't Want You to Know About Lincoln's War!* Spring Hill, TN: Sea Raven Press, 2015.

———. *Slavery 101: Amazing Facts You Never Knew About America's "Peculiar Institution."* Spring Hill, TN: Sea Raven Press, 2015.

———. *Confederate Flag Facts: What Every American Should Know About Dixie's Southern Cross*. Spring Hill, TN: Sea Raven Press, 2016.

———. *Nathan Bedford Forrest and the Ku Klux Klan: Yankee Myth, Confederate Fact*. Spring Hill, TN: Sea Raven Press, 2016.

———. *Seabrook's Bible Dictionary of Traditional and Mystical Christian Doctrines*. Spring Hill, TN: Sea Raven Press, 2016.

———. *Everything You Were Taught About African-Americans and the Civil War is Wrong, Ask a Southerner!* Spring Hill, TN: Sea Raven Press, 2016.

———. *Nathan Bedford Forrest and African-Americans: Yankee Myth, Confederate Fact*. Spring Hill, TN: Sea Raven Press, 2016.

———. *Women in Gray: A Tribute to the Ladies Who Supported the Southern Confederacy*. Spring Hill, TN: Sea Raven Press, 2016.

———. *Lincoln's War: The Real Cause, the Real Winner, the Real Loser*. Spring Hill, TN: Sea Raven Press, 2016.

———. *The Unholy Crusade: Lincoln's Legacy of Destruction in the American South*. Spring Hill, TN: Sea Raven Press, 2017.

———. *Abraham Lincoln Was a Liberal, Jefferson Davis Was a Conservative: The Missing Key to Understanding the American Civil War*. Spring Hill, TN: Sea Raven Press, 2017.

———. *All We Ask is to be Let Alone: The Southern Secession Fact Book*. Spring Hill, TN: Sea Raven Press, 2017.

———. *The Ultimate Civil War Quiz Book: How Much Do You Really Know About America's Most Misunderstood Conflict?* Spring Hill, TN: Sea Raven Press, 2017.

———. *Rise Up and Call Them Blessed: Victorian Tributes to the Confederate Soldier, 1861-1901*. Spring Hill, TN: Sea Raven Press, 2017.

———. *Victorian Confederate Poetry: The Southern Cause in Verse, 1861-1901*. Spring Hill, TN: Sea Raven Press, 2018.

———. *Confederate Monuments: Why Every American Should Honor Confederate Soldiers and Their Memorials*. Spring Hill, TN: Sea Raven Press, 2018.

———. *The God of War: Nathan Bedford Forrest as He Was Seen by His Contemporaries*. Spring Hill, TN: Sea Raven Press, 2018.

———. *The Battle of Spring Hill: Recollections of Confederate and Union Soldiers.* Spring Hill, TN: Sea Raven Press, 2018.

———. *I Rode With Forrest! Confederate Soldiers Who Served With the World's Greatest Cavalry Leader.* Spring Hill, TN: Sea Raven Press, 2018.

———. *The Battle of Nashville: Recollections of Confederate and Union Soldiers.* Spring Hill, TN: Sea Raven Press, 2018.

———. *The Battle of Franklin: Recollections of Confederate and Union Soldiers.* Spring Hill, TN: Sea Raven Press, 2018.

———. *A Rebel Born: The Screenplay* (for the film). Written 2011. Franklin, TN: Sea Raven Press, 2020.

———. (ed.) *A Short History of the Confederate States of America* (Jefferson Davis, Belford Company, NY, 1890). A Sea Raven Press Reprint. Spring Hill, TN: Sea Raven Press, 2020.

———. (ed.) *Prison Life of Jefferson Davis: Embracing Details and Incidents in his Captivity, With Conversations on Topics of Public Interest* (John J. Craven, Sampson, Low, Son, and Marston, London, UK, 1866). A Sea Raven Press Reprint. Spring Hill, TN: Sea Raven Press, 2020.

———. *What the Confederate Flag Means to Me: Americans Speak Out in Defense of Southern Honor, Heritage, and History.* Spring Hill, TN: Sea Raven Press, 2021.

———. *Heroes of the Southern Confederacy: The Illustrated Book of Confederate Officials, Soldiers, and Civilians.* Spring Hill, TN: Sea Raven Press, 2021.

———. *Support Your Local Confederate: Wit and Humor in the Southern Confederacy.* Spring Hill, TN: Sea Raven Press, 2021.

———. *America's Three Constitutions: Complete Texts of the Articles of Confederation, Constitution of the United States of America, and Constitution of the Confederate States of America.* Spring Hill, TN: Sea Raven Press, 2021.

———. *Vintage Southern Cookbook: 2,000 Delicious Dishes From Dixie.* Spring Hill, TN: Sea Raven Press, 2021.

———. *The Bittersweet Bond: Race Relations in the Old South as Described by White and Black Southerners.* Spring Hill, TN: Sea Raven Press, 2022.

———. (ed.) *The Rise and Fall of the Confederate Government* (Jefferson Davis, D. Appleton, New York, 1881). 2 vols. A Sea Raven Press Facsimile Reprint. Spring Hill, TN: Sea Raven Press, 2022.

———. *Secrets of Celebrity Surnames: An Onomastic Dictionary of Famous People.* Cody, WY: Sea Raven Press, 2023.

———. *I, Confederate: Why Dixie Seceded and Fought in the Words of Southern Soldiers.* Spring Hill, TN: Sea Raven Press, 2023.

———. *Twelve Years in Hell: Victorian Southerners Expose the Myth of Reconstruction, 1865-1877.* Cody, WY: Sea Raven Press, 2023.

———. *Seabrook's Complete Battle Book: The War Between the States, 1861-1865.* Cody, WY: Sea Raven Press, 2023.

———. *The Hampton Roads Conference: The Southern View.* Cody, WY: Sea Raven

Press, 2024.

———. *Rocky Mountain Equines: A Photographic Collection of Horses, Donkeys, and Mules of the American West*. Cody, WY: Sea Raven Press, 2024.

———. *Rocky Mountain Bison: A Photographic Collection of Bison of the American West*. Cody, WY: Sea Raven Press, 2024.

———. *Mysterious Invaders: Twelve Famous 20th-Century Scientists Confront the UFO Phenomenon*. Cody, WY: Sea Raven Press, 2024.

———. *We Called Him Jeb: James Ewell Brown Stuart as He Was Seen by His Contemporaries*. Cody, WY: Sea Raven Press, 2024.

———. *Your Soul Lives Forever: Documented Victorian Case Studies Proving Consciousness Survives Death*. Cody, WY: Sea Raven Press, 2024.

———. *Authentic Victorian Ghost Stories: Genuine Early Reports of Apparitions, Wraiths, Poltergeists, and Haunted Houses*. Cody, WY: Sea Raven Press, 2024.

———. *The Greatest Jesus Mystery of All Time: Where Was Christ Between the Ages of 12 and 30?* Cody, WY: Sea Raven Press, 2024.

———. *Vitamin D: The Miracle Treatment for Nearly Every Disease and Health Issue*. Cody, WY: Sea Raven Press, 2024.

———. *Manmade: Male Inventors Who Created the Modern World*. Cody, WY: Sea Raven Press, 2025.

———. *The Way of Holiness: The Story of Religion and Mythology, from the Cave Bear Cult to Christianity—A Study of the Origins, Development, Functions, Symbols, and Themes of Spiritual Thought*. Unpublished manuscript.

———. *Mothers and Bachelors: Ending the Battle of the Sexes—A New Approach to Marriage and the Family Based on the Sciences of Anthropology, Primatology, and Sociobiology*. Unpublished manuscript.

———. *Seabrook's Encyclopedia of Religion and Myth: A Comparative Guide to the Major Beliefs, Deities, People, and Legends of the World's Religions*. Unpublished manuscript.

———. *Families Around the World: A Children's Guidebook to the Marriages and Families of Different Cultures*. Unpublished manuscript.

———. *The True Legend of King Arthur: The Magical Story of Britain's Most Famous Ruler*. Unpublished manuscript.

———. *Glimpses of Heaven: A Guidebook to the Near-Death Experience*. Unpublished manuscript.

———. *Rowena: The Cat Who Wanted to be a Person*. Unpublished manuscript.

———. *Blackie: The Crow Who Was Afraid of Heights*. Unpublished manuscript.

Shedd, William G. T. *Orthodoxy and Heterodoxy: A Miscellany*. New York: Charles Scribner's Sons, 1893.

Sinker, Robert. *The Characteristic Differences of the New Testament from the Immediately Preceding Jewish, and the Immediately Succeeding Christian Literature, Considered as Evidence of the Divine Origin of the New Testament*. Cambridge, UK: Deighton, Bell, and Co., 1865.

Smith, Andrew Phillip. *The Secret History of the Gnostics: Their Scriptures, Beliefs and Traditions.* London, UK: Watkins Publishing, 2017.

Strauss, David Friedrich. *The Life of Jesus, Critically Examined.* New York: Calvin Blanchard, 1860.

Strong, James. *Strong's Exhaustive Concordance of the Bible.* 1894. Nashville, TN: Abingdon Press, 1975 ed.

Taylor, Charles. *The Oxyrhynchus Logia and the Apocryphal Gospels.* Oxford, UK: Clarendon Press, 1899.

Trompfe, Garry W., Gunner B. Mikkelsen, and Jay Johnston (eds.). *The Gnostic World.* London, UK: Routledge, 2019.

U.S. Army Ordnance Center and School. *Radiological Safety Handbook.* Aberdeen Proving Ground, MD: U.S. Government Printing Office, 1976.

Valantasis, Richard. *The Gospel of Thomas.* London, UK: Routledge, 1997.

Walker, Alexander. *Apocryphal Gospels, Acts, and Revelations.* Edinburgh, Scotland: T. and T. Clark, 1870.

Walker, Barbara G. *The Women's Dictionary of Symbols and Sacred Objects.* San Francisco, CA: Harper and Row, 1988.

Weigall, Arthur. *The Paganism in Our Christianity.* New York: G. P. Putnam's Sons, 1928.

Wells, G. A. *The Historical Evidence for Jesus.* Buffalo, NY: Prometheus Books, 1988.

Wilson, John. *Scripture Proofs and Illustrations of Unitarianism.* London, UK: R. Hunter, 1833.

Yogananda, Paramhansa. *Autobiography of a Yogi.* New York: Philosophical Library, 1946.

———. *The Second Coming of Christ: The Resurrection of the Christ Within You.* 2 vols. Los Angeles, CA: Self-Realization Fellowship, 2004.

Zinner, Samuel. *The Gospel of Thomas: In the Light of Early Jewish, Christian, and Islamic Esoteric Trajectories.* London, UK: Matheson Trust, 2011.

The Christ enthroned.

INDEX

INCLUDES TOPICS, PEOPLE, KEYWORDS, KEY PHRASES, & SPELLING VARIATIONS

12 Apostles, 21, 44, 48, 73
abbreviations, 17
academics, 33
account, 25, 124
accretions, 17
acroamatic, 24
adages, 18
Adam (Bible), 94, 107
Adams, John, 45
ADD, 22
additions, 17
African-Americans, 129
age, 41, 126
agrapha, 34
agraphon, 34
allegories, 72
Alogi, 44
alternative health, 151
alternative health and fitness, 151
Ambrose, Saint, 37
America, 6, 128, 130, 150
American Civil War, 3, 129, 151
American history, 3
American politics, 3
American slavery, 129
American South, 3, 129
Americans, 129, 130
ancient Christian Church, 28, 49
ancient Egypt, 9, 16, 25, 30, 44, 74, 124, 126
ancient Egyptian ankh, 28
ancient history, 3
ancient texts, 16
angel, 54, 81
angels, 65, 70, 108
anger, 46
annunciation, 46, 48
Antarctica, 151
anthropology, 131
anti-evangelical representations, 25

aphorisms, 18, 34
Apocalypse of Peter, 29
apocryphal gospels, 25, 26, 123, 125, 132
Apostles, 21, 42, 44, 48, 70, 73, 128
apothegms, 18
apotheosis, 44, 46
Appalachia, 151
Appalachian heritage, 151
apparitions, 131
aquarist, 151
Aquinas, Thomas, 37
Aramaic, 15, 69
arcane, 11, 24, 149
army, 72, 132
art, 6, 125, 126
Articles of Confederation, 128, 130
artisan, 151, 152
artist, 149, 151, 152
artists, 151
ascension, 46, 48
Asian Paganism, 24
Asian traditions, 21
astrological signs, 49
astrological star signs, 73
astrology, 32, 73, 75
astronomical prophecy, 47
astronomy, 151
atheist, 71
Atkins, Chet, 151
attack, 56, 85
audience, 15, 25, 27, 35, 41
authentic Christianity, 25
authentic spirituality, 95
author, 3, 5, 9, 15-17, 22, 29, 35, 41, 125, 149-151
authorship, 15, 21
back, 6, 34, 43, 49, 54, 56, 62, 63, 66, 78, 80, 85, 101, 110
band leader, 151

baptism, 48
Basilica, 37
basket, 58, 90
bass player, 151
battle, 128-131
Battle of Franklin, 128, 130
Battle of Spring Hill, 130
Bede, 37
Behnesa, Egypt, 16
Belgium, 126
believers, 71
bell, 131
Bible, 20, 24, 27, 29, 31, 32, 44, 48, 69-73, 93, 117, 123, 128, 129, 132, 149, 151, 153
Bible authority, 151
Bible canon, 27
Bible studies, 151
biography, 3, 128, 151
birds, 53, 54, 56, 65, 72, 78, 80, 85, 107
birth, 29, 30, 46, 48, 49, 63, 83, 103
bison, 131
blasphemers of the truth, 29
blasphemy, surrounding Jesus, 45
blind, 37, 57, 58, 88, 90
blood, 128
bodies, 71, 89, 96, 108
body, 57, 64, 65, 71, 83, 84, 89, 99, 106, 108, 112, 152
Bolling, Edith, 151
book, 6, 11, 16, 17, 20-22, 24, 25, 27, 29-31, 34, 39-41, 45, 47, 48, 69-75, 102, 123, 125, 127-130, 149-151, 153
book cover designer, 151
book designer, 151
book formatter, 151
Book of Acts, 34, 125
Book of Esdras (second), 47
Book of Hebrews, 41
books, 3, 6, 11, 18, 22, 24, 47, 93, 123-127, 132, 149-153
Boone, Pat, 151
bountiful crops, 49
bows, 59, 95
boy, 41
boyhood, 48
boys, 128
brain, 45, 71

bread, 44, 66, 110
bread sacrament, 44
brother, 21, 57, 87
brothers, 61, 63, 66, 97, 103, 111
bubbling spring, 55, 82
Buchanan, Patrick J., 151
Buddhism, 70
businessman, 151
cabalistic, 24
Caesar, Emperor Tiberius, 111
Campbell, Joseph, 151
Canon, 26, 27
canonical, 16, 21, 24, 26, 31, 32, 34, 38, 39, 46-48, 70, 73, 123, 124
canonical Gospelers, 32
canonical gospels, 26, 31, 32, 34, 38, 39, 47, 48, 124
Capernaum, Israel, 41
Carnton Plantation, 127
Carson, Martha, 151
cartoonist, 151
Cash, Johnny, 151
cast out demons, 44
cat, 131
Catherine of Siena, 24
Catholic Church, 44
cattle, 67, 112
cavalry, 130
caves, 28
Chaldea, 47
character, 25, 42, 44
child, 49, 53, 59, 78, 86, 94, 151
child of light, 72
child of Virgo, 49
child prodigy, 151
children, 36, 53, 56-58, 60, 67, 71, 78, 85, 86, 88, 91, 96, 97, 113
children of humanity, 57, 67, 88, 113
children of light, 71
children's books, 151
Christ, 7, 12, 21, 26, 27, 30, 40, 42, 46, 47, 69-71, 77-116, 123-126, 128, 131, 132, 153
Christ Consciousness, 12, 69, 70, 77-116
Christ is all, 72
Christ is in you, 71
Christ Jesus, 42
Christendom, 26
Christian, 3, 5, 6, 11, 15, 20-22,

24-32, 34, 35, 39, 42-44, 46-49, 69, 71-74, 76, 86, 123-126, 128, 129, 131, 132, 151, 153
Christian Church, 25, 28-30, 39, 46, 49
Christian churches, 21
Christian communities, 35
Christian cross, 28
Christian cult, 30, 126
Christian cults, 43
Christian group, 15
Christian history, 6, 151
Christian idolatry, 48
Christian intellectuals, 25
Christian mystic, 24, 27, 42, 69, 72, 76
Christian mysticism, 3, 11, 28, 71, 74
Christian mystics, 72
Christian pantheist, 15
Christian scripture, 72
Christian traditionalists, 27
Christian world, 74
Christianity, 9, 11, 21, 22, 24-26, 28-32, 39, 45-47, 49, 51, 69, 70, 73, 75, 92, 112, 123-125, 127, 132, 153
Christianization, 29, 44, 45
Christians, 28-30, 39, 43, 44, 46, 48, 70, 71, 92, 112
Christmas, 29, 45, 73, 75, 127, 153
Christmas tree, 29
Christolatry, 47
Christology, 15
Christus, 11, 30
church, 25, 26, 28-30, 39, 44-46, 49, 83, 124, 125
churches, 21, 126
ciphers, 72
circumcision, 60, 97
city, 16, 17, 58, 90
Civil War, 3, 127-129, 151
classical composer, 151
classical history, 17
Clement of Rome, 34
Cleopas, 147
clergy, 24
cloth, 60, 95
clothes, 58, 64, 91, 105
coal, 151
coat, 60, 95

codex, 16, 17, 20, 28
codex format, 20
Codex II, 28
Codex III, 28
Codex IV, 28
codices, 18, 28
coffee, 3
coffee table books, 3
collection, 18, 20, 25, 27, 31, 34, 37, 124, 131
collier, 127
cologne, 48
columns, 14
combs, 151
Combs, Bertram T., 151
comparative mythology, 3, 151
comparative religion, 3, 151
compass, 32
composer, 151
Confederacy, 129, 130, 151
Confederate, 127-130, 151
Confederate flag, 129, 130
Confederate government, 130
Confederate soldiers, 129, 130, 151
Confederate States, 128, 130
Confederate States of America, 128, 130
Confederate veterans, 151
confederation, 128, 130
confirmation bias, 74, 94
conformists, 82
confusion, 77
Congress, 6
consciousness, 12, 69, 70, 72, 77-116, 123, 131
conservationist, 151
Conservatives, 151
Constantine the Great, 39
constellation, 73
constellations, 49, 75
Constitution, 125, 128, 130, 151
Constitution of the Confederate States, 128, 130
content creator, 151
contradictions, 17
contradictory material, 15
conundrums, 15
conventional Christian scholarship, 25
conventional Christianity, 24, 30
conventional Christians, 39, 92

conventions, 6
cooking, 3
Coptic Gospel of Thomas, 18
Coptic texts, 17
Coptic version, 15
corpse, 61, 98, 99
corruption, 8, 29
Cosmic Consciousness, 70, 123
Council of Nicaea, 39
Cowper, Benjamin H., 25
Crawford, Cindy, 151
creative, 28, 70, 71, 78, 88, 91-93, 96, 106, 107, 112, 151
Creative Intelligence, 28, 70, 78, 88, 91-93, 96, 106, 107, 112
creeds, 151
crescent moon, 73
crops, 49
crown of 12 stars, 73
crucifixion, 48
Cruise, Tom, 151
crux ansata, 28
cryptonyms, 72
CT, 125
current, 34, 46, 81
Cyril, Saint, of Jerusalem, 37
Cyrus, Miley, 151
darkness, 57, 62, 87, 99
David, 42, 123, 124, 132, 149
Day of Judgement, 98
Dead Sea Scrolls, 124
death, 3, 21, 30, 31, 34, 39, 44, 46, 48, 49, 53, 56, 65, 68, 72, 77, 83, 84, 96, 99, 107, 108, 115, 131
death on the cross, 48
December 25, 44
defense, 127, 130
deification, 47
deification of Jesus, 47
deletions, 17
designer, 151
desk, 149
development, 131
devices, 72
Didymus the Blind, 37
diet, 3, 151
diet and nutrition, 3, 151
dimensions, 19, 23
dinner, 62, 100, 101

Disciples, 35, 53-61, 63, 66, 68, 70, 73, 79, 81, 84-87, 91, 93, 96, 97, 99, 103, 111, 115
discrimination, 26
disease, 131
disguised heresy, 26
dishonesty, 98
disorder, 22
divine, 28, 44, 45, 58, 70, 78, 81, 85, 87-89, 92, 93, 95, 97, 100, 103-107, 112, 114, 116, 128, 131, 153
Divine Creative Intelligence, 70, 88, 92, 93
Divine Self, 95
divinity, 43, 69, 71, 77, 100, 103, 112
division, 83
Dixie, 130
docent, 151
Docetics, 22, 44
doctor, 58, 89
documents, 20, 35, 46, 123, 149
dog, 67, 112
dogs, 66, 109
donations, 53, 55, 79, 82
door, 26, 64, 69, 104, 110
doors, 74
doublets, 17
doubting Thomas, 21
dove, 92
doves, 59, 92
drummer, 151
drunk, 55, 57, 81, 88
duplications, 17
Duvall, Robert, 151
dying, 49
$E = mc^2$, 72
eagle scout, 151
Earl of Oxford, 151
Early Christian Church, 39, 46
ears, 54, 56, 57, 62, 63, 66, 73, 80, 85, 87, 100, 102, 110
earth, 40, 42, 43, 54, 55, 59, 65, 68, 71, 72, 81, 83, 85, 88, 91, 93, 94, 96, 98, 106-109, 115
Easter, 45
Ebionites, 22, 44
eccentricities, 17
Ecclesia, 39

ecclesiastical institution, 30
Eckhart, Meister, 24
ecumenical mystics, 70
editor, 22, 33-35, 151
editorial designer, 151
EDS, 125, 126, 132
education, 3
educators, 126, 151
Egypt, 9, 16-19, 21, 23, 25, 30, 33, 44, 47, 48, 51, 74, 123, 124, 126
Egyptian, 15-17, 28, 46, 47, 49, 51, 123, 124
Egyptian city, 16
Egyptian Gnosticism, 28
Egyptian Goddess, 28
Egyptian peasants, 17, 51
Einstein, Albert, 72
El-Bahnasa, Egypt, 16
elements, 26, 34
elite audience, 25
elite group, 15
Ellicott, Bishop, 26
emblems, 72
emendations, 17
Emerson, Ralph W., 45
encyclopedist, 151
energy, 72, 80, 86, 91, 96, 105, 107, 109
engineer, 151
English, 11, 25, 76, 123, 124, 127
enigmas, 3, 15
enlightened individuals, 44, 45
enlightenment, 70, 80, 82, 95, 99, 100
entertainment, 151
entrepreneur, 151
Eostre (goddess), 45
epigrams, 18
epiphany, 48
equinoxes, 32
errors, 45, 51, 76, 84
esoteric, 15, 25, 30, 39, 48, 70, 72, 73, 76, 93, 132
esoteric Christian sects, 30
esoteric doctrines, 72
esoterica, 24
Essenes, 22
Essenic-like Christian sects, 30
established Christianity, 30

eternal life, 44, 71, 115
eternality, 85
eternity, 72
ethnic studies, 3
etymologist, 151
etymology, 3, 151
Europe, 45
European history, 3
European royalty, 151
Eusebius, 21, 37, 46
Evelyn-White, Hugh G., 18, 31, 34
evil, 29, 59, 80, 91, 94, 106
evolution, 123
excavation, 17
experience, 37, 48, 73, 84, 91, 106, 131
experiences, 93, 94
extracanonical works, 37
extraction, 32
eye, 55, 57, 79, 82, 83, 86-88, 116, 150
eyes, 57, 59, 73, 86, 87, 94, 115
fables, 25, 72
face, 53, 55, 65, 79, 83, 109
fall equinox, 49
family, 3, 42, 83, 97, 111, 112, 131, 151, 152
family histories, 3
family of David, 42
fans, 151
fast, 53, 55, 57, 67, 79, 82, 88, 113
fasting, 113
Father, 29, 41-45, 53, 55, 57, 59-64, 66, 67, 70, 71, 74, 78, 83, 85, 88, 89, 92, 93, 96, 97, 99, 101, 103, 105, 107, 108, 111, 113-115, 128, 151
Fathers' kingdom, 61, 98
Feast of the Passover, 41
fecundity of water, 28
female, 28, 56, 57, 86, 87, 112
female deity, 28
Female Principle, 112
field, 56, 67, 68, 85, 114, 122
figs, 59, 94
film, 3, 130, 151
film composer, 151
filmmaker, 151
filter, 24
Findlay, Arthur, 21

fire, 54, 55, 65, 80, 82, 83, 106
first Christians, 30, 71
fish, 28, 53, 54, 72, 78-80, 150
fisher, 54, 79, 80, 126
flavorings, 28
flesh, 57, 68, 88, 89, 115
flight into Egypt, 48
flour, 66, 110
food, 53, 79, 112
foolish traditions, 25, 26
foot, 57, 86
Foote, Shelby, 151
footsteps, 21
force, 58, 90, 102, 112, 116
foundations, 30, 124
Founding Father, 128
four quarter signs (astrology), 32
foxes, 65, 107
fragments, 16-18, 20, 21, 31, 48
Francis, Saint, 24
fraud, 26, 47
freedom, 45
fruit, 34, 54, 56, 59, 62, 63, 80, 85, 93, 94, 100, 101
Galatians, letter to the, 73
Galilee, Israel, 41
gastronomy, 151
Gayheart, Rebecca, 151
Gelasian Decree, 37
genealogist, 151
genealogy, 3, 41, 151
genuine Gospels, 25
Germany, 48
ghost, 3, 127, 131
ghost stories, 3, 127, 131
glyphs, 72
gnosis, 30, 47, 71, 76, 90, 92, 102
Gnostic Christian, 15, 29, 73
Gnostic Christians, 48
Gnostic groups, 22
Gnostic principles, 39
Gnostic text, 29
Gnosticism, 28, 30, 31, 125
God, 28, 29, 39, 40, 42-45, 49, 66, 69-73, 77, 78, 81-83, 87, 91, 99-101, 104, 106, 111, 114, 129
God is all mind, 71
God is light, 71
God Realization, 71, 82
goddesses, 89

godhood, 85
gods, 29, 32, 72, 89, 123
gold, 66, 111, 151
Good Shepherd, 39
Gospel, 1, 5, 6, 9, 11, 12, 15-18, 20-22, 24-35, 37-40, 44, 46, 48, 49, 51, 53, 69, 70, 73, 74, 76, 77, 123-126, 128, 132, 153
Gospel of Jesus, 124
Gospel of John, 21, 32, 44, 123
Gospel of Luke, 32, 40
Gospel of Mark, 16, 32, 38, 126
Gospel of Matthew, 32, 73
Gospel of Q, 15, 27, 31, 34, 35, 40, 69, 128, 153
Gospel of Thomas, 1, 6, 9, 11, 12, 15, 16, 18, 20-22, 24-29, 31-35, 37-40, 48, 49, 51, 53, 69, 70, 73, 74, 76, 77, 124-126, 132
government, 130, 132
governor, 151
grain, 54, 80
grapevine, 59, 92
graphic artist, 151
graphic designer, 151
grave, 45
graves, 125, 151
Graves, Robert, 151
Greece, 123
Greek, 15, 17, 18, 20, 21, 28, 29, 33, 71, 76, 123
Greek Gnosticism, 28
Greek prayers, 29
Greek version, 15
Gregory, Saint, 24
Grenfell, Bernard P., 16, 17, 20, 31, 34, 39, 48
Griffith, Andy, 151
guilt, 55, 82
guitarist, 151
gun, 128, 151
gun rights advocate, 151
Hall of Karnak, 14
Hampton Roads Conference, 130
hand, 16, 20, 42, 55-57, 59, 62, 66, 83, 85, 86, 92, 100, 111, 151
hands, 58, 90, 149
happiness, 100, 104, 115, 128, 153
Harding, William G., 151
Harnack, Adolf von, 33, 35

Harris, Rendel, 33
hate, 53, 59, 61, 67, 79, 93, 97, 112
haunted, 127, 131
haunted houses, 131
heading, 30
healed the sick, 44
healer, 40, 69
healing, 43
healing powers, 43
health, 3, 128, 131, 151, 153
health and fitness, 3, 151
heart, 39, 59, 73, 90, 94, 97, 102, 149, 151
hearts, 57, 63, 86, 88, 103
heathen emblem, 28
heaven, 20, 27, 40, 41, 44, 53, 54, 56, 59, 61, 68, 70, 73, 74, 78-81, 85, 86, 88, 89, 92-94, 97-101, 105-107, 110-112, 115, 116, 122, 131
Hebrew, 15
hell, 128, 130
Hermetic Christian sects, 30
hero, 127
heterodox Christianity, 28
heterodoxy, 29, 131
Higher Selves, 70
Hildegard of Bingen, 24
Hinduism, 70
Hindus, 72
Hippolytus, 22, 37
historian, 11, 27, 149-151
historical Jesus, 38, 49, 123, 126, 127
history, 3, 6, 16, 17, 25, 32, 42, 47, 123, 125, 127, 130, 132, 149-151
history museum docent, 151
Holy Book, 72
holy cross, 44
holy figures, 72
Holy Spirit, 59, 93
Holy Trinity, 89, 93
horses, 59, 95, 131
Horus (god), 46, 47
house, 41, 55, 56, 58, 60, 62, 63, 66, 83, 85, 89, 90, 95, 101, 103, 111, 127
houses, 131
humanity, 40, 45, 48, 57, 65, 67, 70, 88, 103, 107, 113

humans, 108
humor, 3, 130, 151
hunt, 16-23, 31, 33-35, 39, 48, 125
Hunt, Arthur S., 16, 17, 20, 31, 34, 39, 48
hunter, 132
hunting, 123
Hymenaeus, 30
I AM, 12, 24, 29, 32, 34, 43, 59, 64, 70, 71, 76, 93, 99, 100, 104, 105, 149
icons, 72
ideograms, 72
idolatry, 48
IF, 15, 20, 22, 24, 30, 32, 34, 37-40, 43, 46, 47, 53, 55-57, 61-63, 65, 67, 71, 76, 78, 82-90, 97-99, 103, 105, 107, 110, 113, 153
ignorance, 46, 85, 90
image of God, 72
images, 6, 65, 107
immortal, 26, 72, 83
immortal light energy, 72
impure, 90
inanimate objects, 84
incarnation, 98, 99, 106
independent thinkers, 84
India, 21, 124, 125
individuals, 18, 24, 37, 44, 45, 76, 82, 83, 87, 93, 95, 97, 98, 102, 104, 113
individuation, 70, 78, 113, 116
Infancy Gospel of Thomas, 22, 25, 26
information, 38, 89, 151
ink, 151
inner divinity, 69, 71, 112
instrument, 151
intellectual, 6
intelligence, 28, 70, 71, 78, 81, 88, 91-93, 96, 106, 107, 112
interpolations, 17
intracanonical material, 37
intuition, 16, 79, 80, 82, 90, 93, 100, 102, 110
inventor, 151
Ireland, 127
Irenaeus, Saint, 32, 37, 39
Isis (goddess), 28
Italy, 21, 123

Jainism, 70
James, 21, 31, 40, 54, 81, 123, 125-127, 131, 132
Jefferies, Richard, 151
Jefferson Davis Historical Gold Medal, 151
Jefferson, Thomas, 45
Jehovah (god), 29
Jerome, Saint, 37
Jerusalem temple, 48
Jesuine biographical material, 37
Jesus, 1, 5, 6, 12, 15-27, 29-49, 51, 53-100, 102-116, 122-128, 131, 132, 147, 153
Jesus Christ, 26, 27, 47
Jesus movement, 35
Jesus Oracles of Oxyrhynchus, 35
Jesus' birth, 29
Jew, 21, 42
jewelry, 151
jewelry designer, 151
jewelry maker, 151
Jewish groups, 22
Jewish-Christian groups, 22
Jewish-Christian sects, 30
Jews, 20, 42, 43, 48
John of the Cross, 24
John the Baptist (Bible), 94
John, Saint, 24, 34, 37, 38, 71
Johns Hopkins University, 124
Joseph, 41, 47, 124, 127, 151
Joses, 40
Jowett, Benjamin, 46
joy, 87, 122
Judah, 42
Judaism, 39, 48, 70
Judas, 21, 40, 53, 77
Judd, Ashley, 151
Judd, Naomi, 151
Judd, Wynonna, 151
Jude, 21
Judea, 61, 99
Judeans, 59, 93
judge, 34
Julian of Norwich, 24
Jung, Carl, 70
Jupiter, 45
Jupiter (god), 45
Karnak, 14
Kentucky, 151

Kentucky Colonel, 151
Keough, Riley, 151
kick the frame, 72
King James Version, 21
Kingdom of God, 70, 77, 111, 114
Kingdom of God Consciousness, 70
Kingdom of Heaven, 20, 27, 56, 61, 68, 70, 73, 74, 78, 85, 86, 88, 89, 92, 94, 97-101, 105, 106, 110-112, 115, 116, 122
KJV, 20, 117
knowledge, 3, 11, 16, 21, 58, 71, 73, 76, 86, 92, 102, 103, 123, 149, 150
knowledge (gnosis), 30
koan, 40, 74
Kronian Christ, 47
Ku Klux Klan, 129
labeling, 24
lacunae, 17, 51, 76
lake, 33
Lake, Kirsopp, 33
lamb, 61, 99
lamp, 58, 90
land, 55, 74, 82
landscape photographer, 151
language, 15, 17, 73
Latin, 15
law, 3, 6, 21, 24, 41, 46, 48, 72, 74, 92-94, 100, 110, 125, 128, 153
Law of Attraction, 3, 21, 24, 46, 48, 74, 92-94, 100, 110, 128, 153
laws of physics, 95, 113
leaf fragments, 20
leather, 17
lectures, 126
lens, 24
LET, 28, 31, 32, 34, 37, 39, 48, 49, 56, 59, 61, 62, 80, 85-87, 92, 98, 100, 104, 129
lexicographer, 151
liberals, 151
library, 6, 11, 18, 28, 30, 51, 127, 132
Library of Congress, 6
life, 3, 28, 30-32, 37, 40, 44, 46, 47, 49, 53, 61, 67-69, 71, 73, 74, 78, 80, 81, 84, 86, 90, 93, 94, 96, 98, 102-104, 107, 108, 112, 115, 116, 123, 124, 126, 130,

132, 150, 151
life after death, 3
lifestyle, 115
light, 20, 25, 42, 54, 57, 58, 60, 62, 64, 65, 71, 72, 81, 87, 90, 94, 96, 99, 100, 105, 107, 108, 126, 132
Light of Christ, 71
like attracts like, 92
limbs, 84
Lincoln's War, 129
lion, 32, 54, 79
literature, 26, 34, 123, 124, 126, 131
litterateur, 151
livestock, 72
Living One, 58, 60, 61, 68, 91, 96, 98-100, 106, 112, 115, 116
Living Word, 97
location, 15, 17, 96
log, 12, 64, 105
logia, 17-19, 23, 33, 47, 132
Logia Iesou (Grenfell and Hunt), 17
logic, 149
Logiographer, 34, 35
logographs, 72
logoi, 18, 124
Logos, 44
Lord, 17, 35, 38-40, 42, 45, 47, 48, 64, 104, 123, 125
lost years, Jesus', 40
love, 3, 26, 59, 67, 83, 87, 93, 106, 112, 114, 128, 149, 150
Loveless, Patty, 151
Lower Selves, 70
Luke, Saint, 34, 37, 38
luminescence, 71, 87
lyricist, 151
magic, 24, 69
Magna Carta, 128
Magus, Simon, 30
mainline Christianity, 26
mainstream Christianity, 25, 49
mainstream Christians, 28, 92, 112
mainstream Jews, 42
mainstream Judaism, 39
mainstream scholars, 24
male, 40, 56, 57, 72, 86, 87, 131
male inventors, 131
Manichaeans, 22
mankind, 40, 72

manmade rules, 49
manuscript, 16, 21, 22, 49, 131
Mark, Saint, 34, 37, 38
marriage, 131
Marvin, Lee, 151
Mary, Virgin, 40, 73
Maslow, Abraham, 70
mass, 44
Massey, Gerald, 46
master, 43, 44, 62, 63, 100, 101
material form, 72
material plane, 69, 99
materialists, 96
matter, 27, 34, 111
Matthew, Saint, 34, 38, 81
McGavocks, 127
McGraw, Tim, 151
ME, 12, 43, 44, 54, 55, 58, 61-67, 72, 81, 82, 91, 97, 99-103, 105, 106, 108, 111, 112, 114, 130, 149, 150
Mediterranean region, 44
memory, 46
men, 3, 42, 47, 68, 73, 116
merchants, 62, 100, 101
messages, 76
messengers of error, 29
Messiah, 42
Messiah narrative, 39
metaphors, 72
metaphysics, 3
microscope, 24
Middle East, 21, 28
military, 3, 128, 151
military history, 3
military officer, 151
milk, 64, 106
mind is all God, 71
mind of Christ, 70, 77, 81, 83, 84, 86, 87, 91, 93, 96, 103, 105, 106, 109, 114
Minerva (goddess), 45
miracle, 37, 40, 131, 150
miracles, 42, 46, 48
mirror, 107
missing years, of Jesus, 21
Mithras (god), 44
modern Christian Church, 29
modern world, 131
Moksha, 70

money, 62, 66, 68, 100, 110, 114
moon, 73, 75, 125
Mosby, John S., 151
Moses, 41
mother, 40, 41, 61, 66, 67, 97, 111-113, 127, 151
motherhood, 106
mothers, 131
mountain, 58, 60, 90, 95, 131, 151
mountains, 11, 151, 152
mules, 131
music, 151
music producer, 151
musician, 151
musicians, 151
mustard, 56, 85
mysteries, 3, 11, 17, 24, 62, 73, 100, 114, 151
mysteries and enigmas, 3
mystery, 16, 21, 40, 131, 153
mystical Christianity, 9, 11
mystical conversion, 38
mystical framework, 25
mystical Jewish mendicant, 40
mystical language, 73
mystical work, 22, 24, 72
mysticism, 3, 11, 28, 48, 71, 74, 151
myths, 72, 75
Naassenes, 22
Nag Hammadi codices, 28
Nag Hammadi, Egypt, 17, 18
Nathanael, 41
nativity, 48
natural health, 3
natural history, 3, 151
nature, 18, 24, 27, 40, 48, 69, 70, 73, 76, 78, 81, 91, 110, 128, 151, 153
nature preservationist, 151
Nazarenes, 44
Nazareth, Israel, 41
neologist, 151
Neoplatonic Christian sects, 30
Netherlands, 124, 126, 127
New Sayings of Jesus (Grenfell and Hunt), 17
New Testament, 24-27, 30, 31, 34, 37-40, 43, 69, 70, 123-128, 131, 153
New Testament Gospelers, 27

New Thought teacher, 39
New World, 60, 96
New York, 123-127, 130-132
Nicephorus, 37
night, 61, 62, 98, 100
Nirvana, 70
nitrate, 17
nonbelievers, 71
nonreligious frameworks, 70
nontraditional Christians, 29
nontraditional spiritual guide, 39
North, 129, 151
North Carolina, 151
Northerners, 128
Nous, 71
numbers, 72
nutrition, 3, 151
occult, 72, 77
occult figurative representations, 72
Old South, 130
Old Testament, 26, 71, 72
Old Testament apocrypha, 26
oneness with the Divine, 70, 88, 95, 97, 103, 104
only begotten son of God, 39, 69
onomastician, 151
onomastics, 3, 151
opinions, 22, 81, 86
oracles, 20
order, 24, 81, 88
Oregon, 126
organist, 151
organizations, 151
organized Church, 29
Oriental turtle dove, 92
Origen, 24, 37
orthodox Christian, 15, 25, 27, 28, 74
orthodox Christian audience, 27
orthodox Christianity, 30, 49
orthodox Christians, 29
orthodoxy, 29, 48, 131
orthography, 20
Oxyrhynchus Oracles, 35
Oxyrhynchus papyri, 20, 22, 34, 125
Oxyrhynchus, Egypt, 16, 17, 39
Pagan, 28-30, 39, 44-49, 75
Pagan deity, 29
Pagan goddess of spring, 45
Pagan holy day, 29
Pagan motif, 39, 49

Pagan myths, 75
Pagan principle, 44
Pagan roots, 29
Pagan Stoics, 44
Pagan sun deity, 44
Pagan symbol of life, 28
Paganism, 24, 32, 132
Paganization of Jesus, 44, 48
Paganization scheme, 44
Pagans, conversion of, 44
painter, 151
paleographic curiosity, 25
Palestine viper, 92
Panama, 123
Papal church, 26
Papias, 37
papyrus, 16, 17, 123
papyrus fragment, 16, 17
Papyrus Oxyrhynchus 1, 16
Papyrus Oxyrhynchus 654, 17
Papyrus Oxyrhynchus 655, 17
parables, 18, 37, 72, 73, 76
parabolic language, 73
paranormal, 3, 151
Parousia, 49
Parton, Dolly, 151
passion, 48
Patterson, Stephen J., 20
Paul the Deacon, 37
Paul, Saint, 20, 24, 30, 34, 38, 42, 70, 72, 81
peace, 55, 60, 83, 87, 95
pearls, 66, 109
pen, 151
pentagram, 84
percussionist, 151
personal knowledge, 16
personifications, 72
Peter, 42
Peter of Sicily, 37
Peter, Saint, 81
Pharisees, 58, 67, 70, 92, 112
Philetus, 30
Philip, 41
Philip of Side, 37
philosopher, 40, 45, 55, 69, 81
Philosophoumena (Hippolytus), 22
philosophy, 3, 20
photographer, 151
photography, 3, 151

photos, 6
physical bodies, 71, 89
physical body, 71, 83, 84, 112
physical death, 72, 99, 108
physician, 125
physics, 95, 113
pianist, 151
pigs, 66, 109
pillow, 129
pious fraud, 26
pit, 58, 90
plane, 69, 99, 108, 115
plantation, 127
poet, 151
poetry, 3, 129
political parties, 151
politics, 3, 151
poltergeists, 131
polymath, 151
poster artist, 151
poverty, 53, 57, 78, 89
power, 42, 64, 65, 95, 106, 107, 111
powers, 43
pray, 53, 55, 64, 67, 79, 82, 104, 113
pre-Resurrection view, 31
preservationist, 151
presidential history, 3
Presley, Elvis, 151
Presley, Lisa M., 151
priesthood, 42
Priestley, Joseph, 42
primitive Christian communities, 35
primitive collection, 34
procession, 75
proclaimers of evil teachings, 29
prodigy, 151
producer, 151
prophecies, 18, 97
prophecy, 45, 47, 73
prophet, 40, 58, 69, 89
prophets, 41, 42, 60, 65, 73, 96, 108, 128
prosateur, 151
prostitution, 127
protection, 6
provenance, 16
proverbs, 18
pseudonymous works, 32
psychologists, 78
psychology, 70, 71

publisher, 6, 151
publishers, 124
publishing designer, 151
punctuation marks, 17
quiz, 3, 129
ranch hand, 151
Ravensdale, Cassidy, 6
reality, 30, 40, 92
rebirth of the sun, 73
Reconstruction, 130
recording, 151
recording studio mixing engineer, 151
red letters, 29
reference, 3, 31, 71
Refutation of All Heresies (Hippolytus), 22
regulations, 6
religion, 3, 11, 20, 24, 28, 30, 31, 39, 44, 49, 70, 71, 82, 92, 95, 103, 104, 113, 131, 151
religious knowledge, 21
Renaissance Man, 151
repetitions, 17
research, 20, 27, 46, 150
resurrection, 31, 42, 46, 48, 49, 132
revelations, 74, 102, 132
Revolutionary period, 3
Revolutionary War, 151
Revolutionary War soldiers, 151
rhythm guitarist, 151
rhythm mandolinist, 151
rituals, 79, 95
road, 38, 66, 110, 147
road to Damascus, 38
Robinson, James M., 20
rock, 45, 54, 80, 105, 123
rock tomb, 45
Rocky Mountains, 11, 151, 152
Roman Empire, 30
Roman world, 44
Rome, 30, 34, 47, 123
rooftops, 58, 90
root, 54, 59, 80, 92
rubbish mound, 16, 39
Rucker, Edmund W., 151
ruins, 16
ruler, 64, 106, 131
Sabbath, 57, 88
sacrament, 44
sacred scripture, 17

sacred symbol, 44
sacred symbols, 72
sacrificial death, 44
saddle, 128
safety, 132
Salome (Bible), 99
samadhi, 70
Samaritan, 61, 99
sand, 17
Sanskrit, 40
Satan, 70
Satori, 70
Savior of all mankind, 40
sayings, 16-18, 20-22, 24, 31-35, 37, 38, 40, 46, 48, 51, 53, 69, 76, 77, 124-126
Sayings of Our Lord, 17, 125
scholar, 17, 25, 27, 151
scholars, 16-18, 20, 22, 24, 27, 30, 33, 37, 48, 58, 92
scholarship, 16, 25, 34, 150
school, 40, 72, 132
science, 3, 20, 24, 71, 150, 151
scientists, 72, 131, 151
Scotland, 127, 132
Scott, George C., 151
screenwriter, 151
scribal mistakes, 17
scribal notes, 28
scribe, 15
scroll format, 20
sculptor, 151
sea, 5, 6, 43, 53, 54, 72, 78-80, 124, 127-131, 151-153
Sea Raven Press, 5, 6, 127-131, 151-153
Seabrook, Lochlainn, 3, 11, 127, 151, 153
seasons, 32, 49
secession, 129
secret, 24, 30, 47, 53, 54, 77, 79, 98, 124, 126, 132
secret sayings, 24, 53, 77, 124
secrets, 11, 130
seed, 56, 61, 85, 98
seeds, 54, 56, 80, 85
Semitic, 15
Sermon on the Mount, 37, 116
serpents, 59, 92
servant, 59, 62, 63, 95, 100, 101

servants, 56, 84
session player, 151
Sethites, 22
sharecroppers, 63, 101, 102
Shedd, William G. T., 26
sheep, 67, 114
sibylline mysteries, 24
Sicily, 37
sick, 44, 55, 82
signs, 32, 42, 49, 72, 73
Sikhism, 70
Simon, 40
sisters, 61, 97, 151
Skaggs, Ricky, 151
sketch artist, 151
slavery, 129
sleeping, 67, 112
sociobiology, 131
soil, 24, 54, 56, 80, 85
soldier, 129
soldiers, 129, 130, 151
Solemn Utterances of Jesus, 18
solstice tree, 29
Son, 73
Son of God, 39, 44
son of Joseph and Mary, 47
Son of Righteousness, 45
songwriter, 151
Sons of Confederate Veterans, 151
son's annual death and rebirth, 49
soul, 57, 65, 68, 71, 72, 85, 87-90, 97, 99, 108, 115, 131
souls, 86, 98, 106
South, 3, 129, 130, 149, 151
Southern Cause, 129
Southern Confederacy, 129, 130
Southerners, 130
space, 26, 113
speaker, 15, 34, 35
spirit, 57, 59, 60, 68, 79, 83, 89, 93, 97, 99, 113, 115, 116
spirit realm, 99
spirits, 55, 82, 89
spiritual beings, 108
spiritual darkness, 87
spiritual enlightenment, 80, 82, 95
spiritual insight, 21, 79
spiritual insights, 40
spiritual light, 87, 90, 94
spiritual nature, 18

spiritual realm, 74, 115
spiritual treasure, 89, 105, 110
Spiritualism, 3, 21
spiritualist, 21
Spiritualists, 48
spirituality, 3, 11, 95, 127, 151
spiritually evolved, 15
spiritually immature, 91, 93, 94, 99, 102, 104, 109, 115
spiritually mature, 78, 94, 99, 100, 104
spring equinox, 44, 49
spurious narratives, 26
star, 73, 75, 85
stars, 73
state of mind, 40, 69, 70, 81, 83, 84, 91, 97
Stephens, Alexander H., 151
Stoics, 44
stone, 12, 63, 64, 102, 105
storage, 71
Stubbs, William, 11
students, 40
study of the soul, 71
suffering, 92
Sufism, 70
summer, 49, 56, 84
summer solstice, 49
sun, 44, 45, 48, 49, 73, 75
Sun of Righteousness, 45
Sunday, 40, 44
sunshine, 151
Sunshine Sisters, the, 151
sun's sacred day, 44
super intelligence, 71
supernatural, 31, 40, 42, 48, 74, 107
superstition, 46, 47
symbol, 28, 29, 44, 48, 70
symbols, 51, 70, 72, 76, 131, 132
Synagogue, 41
syncretism, 24, 28, 30, 44
Synoptic Gospelers, 38
Synoptic parallels, 34
Syria, 33
Syriac, 15
Tawhid, 70
taxes, 112
Taylor, Charles, 34, 35
teacher, 39, 40, 55, 69, 81
Temple, Jerusalem, 41, 43

Tennessee, 127, 151
Tertullian, 8, 29
text, 5, 6, 9, 15, 17, 27, 29, 31, 35, 39, 40, 48, 51, 69, 76, 77, 126
thanatology, 3
the Left, 24
the North, 129
The South, 149
thealogy, 3
Theodosius, Emperor, 28
Theodotus, 43
theologian, 29
theologians, 24
theological discrepancies, 15
theological position, 15
theological system, 24
theology, 3, 28
theories, 21, 22, 27, 31
Theosis, 49, 70-72, 74, 81, 97, 99, 100, 103
Therapeutae, 22
Thessalonians 1, 38
Thessalonians 2, 38
thieves, 113
Third Ear, 80, 82, 86, 87, 100, 110
Third Eye, 82, 116
Thomas, Didymos Judas, 21
Thomas, Saint, 21, 34, 35, 77, 81, 82
thorns, 54, 59, 80, 94
time, 15, 16, 18, 21, 22, 26, 30, 31, 40, 44, 46, 47, 49, 62, 70, 73, 74, 80, 82, 86, 91, 100, 101, 107, 113, 131, 150, 153
tokens, 72
totems, 72
toy, 86
Transcendendalism, 45
Transfiguration, 48
transpositions, 17
travel, 105
treasure, 59, 64, 67, 68, 89, 94, 104, 105, 110, 114, 122, 128, 150
tree, 29, 59, 93
trees, 56, 84
tribe of Judah, 42
true faith, 8, 29
true light, 71
truth, 27, 29, 30, 45, 48, 64, 71, 74, 77, 78, 88, 90, 91, 103, 105, 114, 149, 150

TV, 151
TV show, 151
U.S. army, 72, 132
U.S. government, 132
unenlightened, 15, 70, 76, 79, 81, 82, 84, 85, 87, 91, 93, 96, 97, 109, 111
unenlightened masses, 15
Union, 6, 130, 151
Union soldiers, 130
Unitarians, 48
United States, 6, 45, 130
United States of America, 6, 130
unity with God, 69, 81
universe, 28, 71, 78, 81, 112
University of Chicago, 123
unorthodox, 29
unorthodox Christianity, 28
unorthodox Christians, 29
Upper Egypt, 17, 21, 35
USA, 5, 6, 11
Valentinians, 22
Valentinus, 24
vegetation cults, 49
vehicles, 71
Victorian Period, 3
videographer, 151
village, 58, 89
vineyard, 62, 63, 101
Virgin, 44, 45, 48, 73
virgin birth, 48
Virgin Mary, 73
Virginia, 151
Virgo, 49, 73
vitamin D, 131
vocalist, 151
voice, 46
voices, 21, 47, 124
walking, 6, 66, 110
walking on water, 6
walls, 28
war, 3, 55, 83, 127-130, 150, 151
War Between the States, 130
War for the Constitution, 151
water, 6, 28, 32
watercolorist, 151
wealth, 57, 65, 89, 107, 128, 153
Web designer, 151
West Virginia, 151
wheat, 61, 98

wife, 151
wildlife, 3, 151
Wilson, Woodrow, 151
wind, 64, 105
wine, 57, 60, 88, 95
wineskins, 60, 95
winter, 29, 44, 49, 56, 73, 84
winter solstice, 29, 44, 49, 73
winter solstice celebration, 29
wisdom, 47, 48, 74, 77, 84, 110, 124, 126
Witherspoon, Reese, 151
witness, 107
Womack, Lee Ann, 151
womb, 45, 64, 105, 106
women, 3, 68, 116, 129
world, 3, 6, 24, 25, 29, 44, 46, 47, 54-57, 60, 61, 64, 68, 71, 74, 80, 81, 83-85, 87, 88, 93, 96, 98, 101, 104, 106, 114, 115, 124, 126, 131, 132, 149, 151
world history, 3
worry, 79
wounds, 49
wrangler, 151
writer, 15, 24, 25, 37, 149, 151
writers, 22, 24, 38, 151
writing, 3, 16, 27, 31, 38, 42, 149-151
Wyoming, 5, 6
Yahweh (god), 29
Yankee myth, 129
yoga, 40
yoke, 40
Zen Buddhism, 40
Zen Buddhist koan, 40
Zen Buddhist masters, 40
Zeus, 29
Zeus (god), 29
zodiacal chart, 49
zookeeper, 151
Zoroastrianism, 44

Jesus and Cleopas on the road to Emmaus.

Praise for Author-Historian-Artist
Lochlainn Seabrook

Comments from our readers around the world

★ "Lochlainn Seabrook is a genius writer!" — STEVEN WARD

★ "Best author ever." — EMILY (last name withheld)

★ "We get asked a lot what books we use and read. We don't do many modern historians, but we make an exception for some, and Lochlainn Seabrook is one of them. His works are completely well researched from original documents, and heavily footnoted and documented." — SOUTHERN HISTORICAL SOCIETY

★ "Looking forward to more Lochlainn Seabrook books, my favourite historian!" — ALBERTO IGLESIAS

★ "Lochlainn Seabrook is one of the finest authors on true history in this century. His books should be on every student's desk." — RONDA SAMMONS RENO

★ "All of Col. Seabrook's books are great. I have bought most of them and want to end up buying them all." — DAVID VAUGHN

★ "Lochlainn pulls together such arcane facts with relative ease, compiling these into ordinary prose that strike to the heart with substance, no fluff-speak. I am awestruck! Really. He is an inspiration to me. . . . He is truly a revolutionist. He dares to speak what others whisper; he writes with a boldness and an authoritative knowledge that is second to none." — JAY KRUIZENGA

★ "Mr. Lochlainn Seabrook is . . . the most well researched and heavily documented author I've ever read. His books are must haves. Everything he writes should be required reading! I assure you, you won't be disappointed. One simply cannot go wrong with his books. Mr. Seabrook is awesome! . . . I have never read any other author as well researched and footnoted as him. I've been in love with Mr. Seabrook for almost 5 years now. His quick wit and logic is enough reason to purchase his books. But the mere fact that he's so extensively researched is icing on the cake. Mr. Seabrook is my favorite, hands down." — LANI BURNETTE RINKEL

★ "My favorite book is the Bible. Lochlainn Seabrook wrote my second favorite book." — RICHARD FINGER

★ "I have a new favorite author and his name is Lochlainn Seabrook." — J. EWING

★ "Lochlainn Seabrook is an incredible writer and I love all of his books on the South. . . . His writing is brilliant. . . . I look forward to reading more of his masterpieces. Thank you." — JOEY (last name withheld)

★ "It's hard to choose just one of Lochlainn's books!" — ROSANNE STEELE

★ "Mr. Seabrook, thank you ever so much for blessing us with your most enlightening works." — LAURENCE DRURY

★ "I recommend anything written by Lochlainn Seabrook." — HOTRODMOB

★ "Awesome books . . . by a great writer of truth, Lochlainn. Thank you so much. Keep up the great work you do." — WILDBUNCH19INF

★ "I love Lochlainn Seabrook's style and approach. It's not the 'norm.' What a miracle his books are. . . . He is a literal life changing author! Amazing books!" — KEITH PARISH

★ "I adore Mr. Seabrook's style and I love his books. I love an author that does proper research, and still finds a way to engage the reader. Mr. Seabrook does an admirable job of both." — DONALD CAUL

★ "Lochlainn Seabrook's books are much more well researched and authoritative than those eminently celebrated as being the authorities on the subjects he writes on. You can always trust to find the truth in his writings. . . . He does not rewrite history, but instead shows it as it is." — GARY STIER

★ "I love all of Colonel Seabrook's books. They are informative and enlightening, and his warm Southern hospitality writing style makes you feel right at home." — KEITH CRAVEN

★ "Lochlainn Seabrook's work is an absolute treasure of scholarship and historic scope." — MARK WAYNE CUNNINGHAM

★ "Mr. Seabrook's command of . . . history is breathtaking. . . . He deserves great renown—check out his books!" — MARGARET SIMMONS

★ "I love Seabrook's writings. LOVE!!! . . . So grateful to know the truth! Keep writing Lochlainn!!!" — REBECCA DALRYMPLE

★ "Lochlainn Seabrook . . . [has] probably [written] the best book on mental science in existence by a living author. Along with Thomas Troward, Emmet Fox, and Jack Addington, Mr. Seabrook is one of the top four mental science authors of all time, since biblical times." - IAN BARTON STEWART

★ "Glad I discovered Mr. Seabrook! . . . He writes eye opening books! Unbelievable the facts he unearths - and he backs it all up with truth, notes, footnotes, and bibliography! . . . He always amazes me! His books always see the whole picture. His timelines and bibliographies are incredible. He always provides carefully reasoned arguments! He's the best. To me I think he's better than the late great Shelby Foote! America needs more like Lochlainn Seabrook. I can't wait to own all of his books on the war someday. Everyone who wants the Truth, who seeks the Truth and wants the full story, should read his books." — JOHN BULL BADER

★ "I love all of Colonel Seabrook's books!" — DEBBIE SIDLE

★ "Lochlainn Seabrook is well educated and versed in what he writes and I'm impressed with the delivery." — THOMAS L. WHITE

★ "Lochlainn Seabrook is the author of great works of scholarship." — JOHN B. (last name withheld)

★ "Thank you Lochlainn Seabrook for your wonderful books! You are the real deal! You are an amazing author and I love your books!!" — SOPHIA MEOW CELLIST

★ "I really enjoy Mr. Seabrook's books! His knowledge is beyond belief!" — SANDRA FISH

★ "Love Lochlainn Seabrook. Awesome!!" — ROBIN HENDERSON ARISTIDES

★ "Kudos to Lochlainn Seabrook who is a very good and informative professional truthful historian. We need more like him!" — AMY VACHON

MEET THE AUTHOR

AMERICAN POLYMATH LOCHLAINN SEABROOK is a bestselling author, award-winning historian, and nationally acclaimed artist. A descendant of the families of Alexander Hamilton Stephens, John Singleton Mosby, Edmund Winchester Rucker, and William Giles Harding, the neo-Victorian scholar is a 7th generation Kentuckian, and one of the most prolific and widely read writers in the world today. Known by literary critics as the "new Shelby Foote," the "American Robert Graves," the "Southern Joseph Campbell," and the "Rocky Mountain Richard Jefferies," and by his fans as the "Voice of the Traditional South," he is a recipient of the United Daughters of the Confederacy's prestigious Jefferson Davis Historical Gold Medal, and is considered the foremost Southern interpreter of American Civil War history—or what he refers to as the War for the Constitution (1861-1865). A lifelong litterateur, the Sons of Confederate Veterans member has authored and edited books ranging in topics from

ancient and modern history, politics, science, comparative religion, diet and nutrition, spirituality, astronomy, entertainment, military, biography, mysticism, photography, and Bible studies, to natural history, technology, paleography, music, humor, gastronomy, etymology, onomastics, mysteries, alternative health and fitness, wildlife, comparative mythology, genealogy, Christian history, and the paranormal; books that his readers describe as "game changers," "transformative," and "life altering."

One of America's most popular living historians, he is a 17th generation Southerner of Appalachian heritage who descends from dozens of patriotic Revolutionary War soldiers and Confederate soldiers from Kentucky, Tennessee, North Carolina, and Virginia. Also a history, wildlife, and nature preservationist, the well-respected scrivener began life as a child prodigy, later maturing into an archetypal Renaissance Man. Besides being cofounder and co-CEO of Sea Raven Press, an accomplished writer, author, historian, biographer, lexicographer, encyclopedist, neologist, publisher, editor, poet, creative, onomastician, etymologist, and Bible authority, the influential prosateur is also a Kentucky Colonel, eagle scout, entrepreneur, businessman, composer, screenwriter, nature, wildlife, and landscape photographer, videographer, and filmmaker, artist, artisan, painter, watercolorist, sculptor, ceramic artist, visual artist, sketch artist, pen and ink artist, graphic artist, graphic designer, book designer, book formatter, editorial designer, book cover designer, publishing designer, Web designer, poster artist, cartoonist, content creator, inventor, aquarist, genealogist, jewelry designer, jewelry maker, former history museum docent, and a former ranch hand, zookeeper, and wrangler. A contemporary songwriter (of some 3,000 songs in a dozen genres), he is also a pianist, organist, drummer, bass player, rhythm guitarist, rhythm mandolinist, percussionist, classical composer, film composer (currently his musical work has been featured in 11 movies), lyricist, band leader, multi-instrument musician, lead vocalist, backup vocalist, session player, music producer, and recording studio mixing engineer, who has worked and performed with some of Nashville's top musicians and singers.

Currently Seabrook is the multi-genre author and editor of over 100 adult and children's books (totaling some 30,000 pages and 15,000,000 words) that have earned him accolades from around the globe. His works, which have sold on every continent except Antarctica, have introduced hundreds of thousands to vital facts that have been left out of our mainstream books. He has been endorsed internationally by leading experts, museum curators, award-winning historians, chart-topping authors, celebrities, filmmakers, noted scientists, well regarded educators, TV show hosts and producers, renowned military artists, venerable heritage organizations, and distinguished academicians of all races, creeds, and colors. He currently holds two world records: He is the author of the most books (12) on American military officer Nathan Bedford Forrest, and he was the first to publicize and describe the 19th-Century platform reversal of America's two main political parties, namely that Civil War era Democrats (primarily in the South—the Confederacy) were Conservatives, while Civil War era Republicans (primarily in the North—the Union) were Liberals.

Of northern, western, and central European ancestry, he is the 6th great-grandson of the Earl of Oxford and a descendant of European royalty through his Kentucky father and West Virginia mother. A proud descendant of Appalachian coal miners, trainmen, mountain folk, and wilderness pioneers, his modern day cousins include: Johnny Cash, Elvis Presley, Lisa Marie Presley, Billy Ray and Miley Cyrus, Patty Loveless, Tim McGraw, Lee Ann Womack, Dolly Parton, Pat Boone, Naomi, Wynonna, and Ashley Judd, Ricky Skaggs, the Sunshine Sisters, Martha Carson, Chet Atkins, Patrick J. Buchanan, Cindy Crawford, Bertram Thomas Combs (Kentucky's 50th governor), Edith Bolling (second wife of President Woodrow Wilson), Andy Griffith, Riley Keough, George C. Scott, Robert Duvall, Reese Witherspoon, Lee Marvin, Rebecca Gayheart, and Tom Cruise.

A constitutionalist, avid outdoorsman, wilderness conservationist, and gun rights advocate, Seabrook is the author of the international blockbuster, *Everything You Were Taught About the Civil War is Wrong, Ask a Southerner!* He lives with his wife and family in the magnificent Rocky Mountains, heart of the American West, where you will find him hiking, filming, and writing.

For more information on Mr. Seabrook visit

LochlainnSeabrook.com

Nurture Your Mind, Body, and Spirit!
READ THE BOOKS OF

SEA RAVEN PRESS

Visit our Webstore for a wide selection of wholesome, family-friendly, evidence-based, educational books for all ages. You'll be glad you did!

Artisan-Crafted Books & Merch From the Rocky Mountains

SeaRavenPress.com

LochlainnSeabrook.com
TheBestCivilWarBookEver.com
YouTube.com/@SeabrookFilms
Rumble.com/user/SeaRavenPress
AmbianceGoneWild.com
Pond5.com/artist/LochlainnSeabrook
RedBubble.com/people/SeaRavenPress/shop

LOCHLAINN SEABROOK ∞ 153

If you enjoyed this book you will be interested in Col. Seabrook's popular related titles:

☛ JESUS AND THE GOSPEL OF Q: CHRIST'S PRE-CHRISTIAN TEACHINGS AS RECORDED IN THE NEW TESTAMENT
☛ SEABROOK'S BIBLE DICTIONARY OF TRADITIONAL & MYSTICAL CHRISTIAN DOCTRINES
☛ CHRIST IS ALL & IN ALL: REDISCOVERING YOUR DIVINE NATURE & THE KINGDOM WITHIN
☛ JESUS & THE LAW OF ATTRACTION: THE BIBLE-BASED GUIDE TO CREATING PERFECT HEALTH, WEALTH, & HAPPINESS
☛ THE GREATEST JESUS MYSTERY OF ALL TIME: WHERE WAS CHRIST BETWEEN THE AGES OF 12 AND 30?
☛ CHRISTMAS BEFORE CHRISTIANITY: HOW THE BIRTHDAY OF THE "SUN" BECAME THE BIRTHDAY OF THE "SON"

Available from Sea Raven Press and wherever fine books are sold

ALL OF OUR BOOK COVERS ARE AVAILABLE AS 11" X 17" POSTERS, SUITABLE FOR FRAMING.

SeaRavenPress.com

www.ingramcontent.com/pod-product-compliance
Lightning Source LLC
Chambersburg PA
CBHW032050150426
43194CB00006B/485